THE PSYCHIC VOYAGE: NAVIGATING THE UNSEEN REALM

A Comprehensive Guide to Developing
Your Psychic Abilities

D.R. T STEPHENS

S.D.N Publishing

CONTENTS

GENERAL DISCLAIMER

This book is intended to provide informative and educational material on the subject matter covered. The author(s), publisher, and any affiliated parties make no representations or warranties with respect to the accuracy, applicability, completeness, or suitability of the contents herein and specifically disclaim any implied warranties of merchantability or fitness for a particular purpose.

The information contained in this book is for

general information purposes only and is not intended to serve as legal, medical, financial, or any other form of professional advice. Readers should consult with appropriate professionals before making any decisions based on the information provided. Neither the author(s) nor the publisher shall be held responsible or liable for any loss, damage, injury, claim, or otherwise, whether direct or indirect, consequential, or incidental, that may occur as a result of applying or misinterpreting the information in this book.

This book may contain references to third-party websites, products, or services. Such references do not constitute an endorsement or recommendation, and the author(s) and publisher are not responsible for any outcomes related to these third-party references.

In no event shall the author(s), publisher, or any affiliated parties be liable for any direct, indirect, punitive, special, incidental, or other consequential damages arising directly or indirectly from any use of this material, which is provided "as is," and without warranties of any kind, express or implied.

By reading this book, you acknowledge and agree that you assume all risks and responsibilities concerning the applicability and consequences of the information provided. You also agree to indemnify, defend, and hold harmless the author(s), publisher, and any affiliated parties from any and all liabilities, claims, demands, actions, and causes of action whatsoever, whether or not foreseeable, that may arise from using or misusing the information contained in this book.

Although every effort has been made to ensure the accuracy of the information in this book as of the date of publication, the landscape of the subject matter covered is continuously evolving. Therefore, the author(s) and publisher expressly disclaim responsibility for any errors or omissions and reserve the right to update, alter, or revise the content without prior notice.

By continuing to read this book, you agree to be bound by the terms and conditions stated in this disclaimer. If you do not agree with these terms, it is your responsibility to discontinue use of this book immediately.

FOUNDATIONS OF PSYCHIC AWARENESS

UNDERSTANDING PSYCHIC ABILITIES

Understanding psychic abilities requires delving into a vast and intricate world where the mind's potential extends beyond the tangible and into realms that have fascinated humanity for centuries. This exploration not only touches on the historical and cultural significance of psychic phenomena but also invites us to open our minds to possibilities that lie at the very edge of science and spirituality.

Psychic abilities, often regarded as the sixth sense, encompass a range of phenomena that include but are not limited to clairvoyance (clear seeing), clairaudience (clear hearing), clairsentience (clear feeling), and intuition. These abilities suggest that individuals can perceive information, sense emotions, or even predict future events in ways that transcend the usual human sensory capabilities. Historically, various cultures and civilizations have recognized and nurtured such abilities, integrating them into their spiritual practices, healing methods, and decision-making processes. Recognizing the potential that lies inside oneself is the first step on the path to developing one's psychic abilities. It is not just a select few people who possess this capacity; rather, it is a dormant skill that is present in every single person. In order to take the first step, one must first tune into their inner self, pay attention to their subtle intuitions, and observe the world with an open mind and a sense of wonder. The key is to acquire the ability to pay attention to the subtle utterances of intuition that lead us on a daily basis, which are sometimes overlooked amidst the chaos of our hectic life.

There has been a lot of discussion and doubt over the scientific interpretation of psychic experiences. In spite of this, there are a great number of reports and verified cases of psychic skills manifesting in a variety of different ways. The area of parapsychology is comprised of researchers who explore these phenomena with the goal of comprehending the mechanisms that underlie psychic experiences and the implications that these experiences have for our comprehension of consciousness and physical reality. Despite the fact that the scientific community is still divided, the fact that there is ongoing interest and investigation in this field suggests that there is a collaborative effort directed toward comprehending the complete range of human experience.

In order to create psychic powers, it is not enough to just acknowledge their presence; rather, it is necessary to take a holistic approach to the process of personal development. The practices that fall under this category are those that attempt to improve mental clarity, emotional equilibrium, and physical well-being. The practices of meditation, mindfulness, and energy work are essential components of this process, as they contribute to the development of an internal environment that is favorable to the growth of psychic skills. In addition, ethical considerations play a significant part, as the development of psychic skills comes with the duty of employing them in a manner that is both smart and kind.

In the process of embarking on this journey, it is essential that we approach the development of our psychic abilities with an open heart and mind, enabling ourselves to investigate the unseen with a sense of wonder and reverence. The journey is not just about obtaining new skills, but also about undergoing a substantial amount of personal transformation. Our preconceptions are called into question, and we are encouraged to embrace a more expansive vision of what it means to be human. It encourages us to go inward. As a result of this exploration, not only are we able to unleash our psychic potential, but we also strengthen our connection to the world that surrounds us. At the same time, we uncover a realm in which spirit and matter converge, and where the unseen also becomes visible.

As we continue our exploration, we will explore more deeply into particular psychic skills, tactics for their development, and the ways in which we might incorporate these abilities into our everyday lives. It is not only about developing psychic abilities, but also about personal development, self-discovery, and connecting with the cosmos in ways that are profound and significant. This trip is about each of these things.

TYPES OF PSYCHIC ABILITIES

The spectrum of psychic abilities is as broad as it is fascinating, encompassing a range of phenomena that defy conventional understanding and open the door to a world beyond the physical senses. Let's delve into the various types of psychic abilities, aiming to provide a comprehensive overview of the skills that have captivated human curiosity and spurred both skepticism and belief throughout history.

With the ability to obtain knowledge about an object, person, location, or physical event through means other than the human senses that are commonly known, clairvoyance, often known as "clear seeing," is possibly the most well recognized psychic gift. Typically, this takes the shape of flashes or detailed sceneries that appear in the mind's eye. Visions of the past, present, or future might be a manifestation of this phenomenon.

Clairaudience, sometimes known as "clear hearing," is a hearing ability that allows certain people to hear sounds, music, or phrases that are not audible to others. In addition to delivering instruction, warnings, or simply messages of comfort and confidence, these aural communications may originate from unseen sources such as the higher self, outside spirits, or another unseen source.

The term "clairsentience," which literally translates to "clear feeling," refers to the intense awareness of feelings and sensations that are not one's own. This awareness provides insights into the feelings and physical well-being of other people. The manifestation of this skill frequently takes the form of gut emotions or innate responses that turn out to be incredibly specific.

The psychic capacity known as intuition is present in all people, albeit to varying degrees to varying degrees. Without the use of conscious reasoning, judgments and perceptions are guided by that "knowing" or feeling that cannot be explained. The development of one's intuition can result in the acquisition of significant insights, and it is frequently the basis upon which is constructed additional psychic skills.

People who have empathy are able to thoroughly sense and occasionally absorb the feelings and energies of other people. Empathy is a sort of psychic sensitivity to others. This skill has the potential to generate profound connections to both people and situations; nevertheless, it requires management in order to avoid becoming overwhelmed.

This idea that an individual's consciousness is completely private is called into question by telepathy, which is the direct transmission of thoughts or sensations between persons without the need of the five traditional senses. Some examples of telepathic experiences include being able to identify the person who is contacting you on the phone and having a profound grasp of the feelings or ideas that another person is not expressing verbally.

Being able to connect with spirits that have left our physical realm is what is meant by the term "mediumship." It is common for mediums to provide closure, messages of love, or evidence that life continues beyond death. They play the role of conduits between the living and the dead.

By touching an object, psychometry allows one to gather information about its energy or history. It is possible for practitioners to obtain impressions about the history of the thing, which may include the prior owners of the piece or any major events related with it.

Individuals who engage in the practice of remote viewing are able to visualize places, things, or people that are not physically visible to them. Several scientific tests have been conducted to investigate this capability, and it has even been utilized in intelligence operations conducted by the military.

When people allow a higher consciousness or spirit to create written material through them without actively writing it down, this is an example of automatic writing, which is a sort of psychic communication. There is a possibility that the outcomes will be artistic inspiration, communications from the spirit realm, or revelations from the subconscious.

The ability to travel outside of the physical body and explore the astral plane or other dimensions is made possible via the practice of astral projection, also known as out-of-body experiences. This technique is frequently associated with substantial personal development, and it has been described in a wide variety of spiritual traditions.

Despite the fact that energy healing is not usually regarded to be a psychic skill, it is characterized by the manipulation of energy fields surrounding the body in order to facilitate healing, balance, and overall well-being. Practitioners have the ability to recognise and affect the energy that is present within and surrounding another individual, which frequently results in tremendous healing on all levels—physical, emotional, and spiritual.

These abilities, among others, offer glimpses into the vast potential of human consciousness and the interconnectedness of all things. Developing these skills requires patience, practice, and an open heart, but for those who embark on this journey, the rewards can be life-changing, offering a deeper understanding of the universe and our place within it.

THE SCIENCE AND SKEPTICISM

Throughout the course of its history, the scientific investigation of psychic phenomena has made its way through a turbulent route, with the mainstream scientific community exhibiting varied degrees of skepticism and acceptance. Parapsychology is a specialized field of study that has arisen in spite of this fact. Its primary objective is to conduct exhaustive research and gain an understanding of the mechanisms that underlie psychic talents and experiences. Let's explore the scientific viewpoint on psychic phenomena, addressing the widespread skepticism that exists regarding these phenomena and highlighting the ongoing attempts that are being made to bridge the gap between the universe of science and the realm of the psychic.

Extrasensory perception (ESP), telekinesis, and the continuation of consciousness after death are all examples of phenomena that are investigated through the science of parapsychology. For the purpose of determining whether or not psychic claims are true, researchers in this discipline have conducted controlled trials and then analyzed the data using statistical methods. In the field of parapsychology, the Ganzfeld experiment is well recognized as one of the most famous experiments. This experiment was developed to test for telepathy. Some investigations have reported results that are much higher than the levels of chance, which suggests the presence of telepathic powers. In order to receive telepathic signals, participants are placed in a state of sensory deprivation.

The lack of a clear, replicable process that is compatible with the current understanding of physics and biology serves as a common source of skepticism regarding psychic occurrences. People who are skeptical about psychic claims believe that they cannot be considered scientifically valid if they do not have proof that is consistent, repeatable, and conducted under controlled conditions. An additional factor that has contributed to the growth of skepticism is the existence of fraudulent and self-deceptive claims about psychic abilities.

A number of intriguing discoveries have been made in spite of these obstacles, which point to the presence of phenomena that science has not yet fully comprehended. During global events, for instance, the Global Consciousness Project has documented statistically significant deviations, which suggests that there may be a probable interconnection of human consciousness on a global scale. This project monitors random number generators all around the world.

In the dispute between those who are skeptical of psychic phenomena and those who are in favor of them, the standards of evidence and the interpretation of data are frequently at the center of the discussion. Proponents of psychic phenomena say that, by their very nature, they may not always correspond to such norms, which necessitates an open-minded approach to inquiry and interpretation. Skeptics ask for results that are rigorous, reproducible, and under conditions that are tightly controlled.

Recent developments in the field of physics, such as quantum entanglement, have provided potential frameworks for comprehending the possible occurrence of psychic events. It is possible that phenomena such as telepathy and remote viewing could have their origins in these theories, which propose that the universe is fundamentally interconnected on a quantum level. These concepts, despite the fact that they

are still hypothetical, constitute a bridge between the study of consciousness and the physical sciences. They give hope for a future in which psychic phenomena can be understood more thoroughly within the context of science.

The investigation of psychic phenomena from a scientific point of view is not merely an academic undertaking; rather, it has serious repercussions for our comprehension of consciousness, the nature of reality, and the capabilities of the human mind. We may one day be able to uncover new depths of human experience and understanding if we continue to investigate these phenomena with an open, critical, and rigorous attitude. This would allow us to transcend the barriers between the seen and the unseen, as well as the known and the unpredictable.

PREPARING THE
MIND AND BODY

MENTAL READINESS

Achieving mental readiness is a pivotal step in honing psychic abilities, as it requires a serene mind and concentrated focus. Let's delve into methods that foster mental clarity, an essential foundation for psychic development.

Cultivating a Meditation Practice

Meditation stands as the cornerstone of psychic development, offering a pathway to profound mental clarity and focus. Regular meditation sessions, tailored to individual needs and preferences, can significantly enhance one's ability to connect with the psychic realm. Techniques such as mindfulness meditation, which emphasizes present-moment awareness, and focused attention meditation, where concentration is directed towards a single point of reference, are particularly effective. These practices help quiet the mind, reduce stress, and increase the capacity for psychic awareness.

Visualization Techniques

Visualization is another powerful tool for psychic development, involving the creation of mental images to sharpen the mind's eye. Practitioners can start with simple exercises, like picturing a familiar object in great detail, then progress to more complex visualizations that incorporate sensory details such as texture, color, and sound. This technique not only enhances clairvoyance but also aids in forming a deeper connection with psychic intuition.

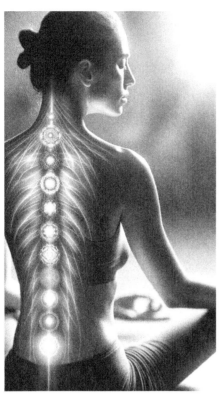

Energy Cleansing and Protection

A clear and protected energy field is essential for maintaining mental clarity. Regularly practicing energy cleansing techniques, such as smudging with sage or using visualization to imagine a protective light surrounding the body, can help remove psychic debris and shield against negative influences. This practice ensures that psychic work is conducted within a safe and clear energetic space, facilitating a stronger, undisturbed focus.

Diet and Physical Health

The connection between physical health and psychic ability is profound. A diet rich in whole foods, especially those high in omega-3 fatty acids, antioxidants, and vitamins, can enhance cognitive function and, by extension, psychic receptivity. Hydration and regular physical exercise also play critical roles in maintaining mental clarity. Incorporating yoga or tai chi, which align physical movement with breath and intention, can further support the connection between body, mind, and spirit.

Sleep and Dream Work

Quality sleep is vital for psychic development, as it allows the mind to rest, reset, and process psychic experiences, often through dreams. Engaging in dream work, such as keeping a dream journal to record and interpret psychic dreams, can provide valuable insights and enhance one's psychic capabilities. Establishing a calming bedtime routine that may include meditation or reading can improve sleep quality and, consequently, mental readiness for psychic work.

Developing Concentration and Focus

Exercises specifically designed to improve concentration and focus can significantly benefit psychic development. Practices like focusing on a candle flame without letting the mind wander or engaging in activities that require sustained attention can strengthen the mental muscles needed for psychic work. Over time, these exercises can help practitioners maintain focus during psychic readings and enhance the accuracy and depth of their insights.

Emotional Balance and Resilience

Emotional clarity is just as important as mental clarity in psychic development. Techniques for managing emotions, such as journaling, therapy, and practicing emotional freedom techniques (EFT), can help clear emotional blockages. A balanced emotional state supports a clear psychic channel, allowing for more accurate readings and a deeper understanding of intuitive messages.

Mindfulness and Present-Moment Awareness

Incorporating mindfulness into daily life can greatly enhance mental clarity. Being fully present in each moment, whether in mundane tasks or during meditation, trains the mind to focus and stay attuned to the intuitive process. This awareness can make it easier to access psychic abilities on demand and integrate psychic insights into everyday decision-making.

By dedicating time and effort to these practices, individuals can develop a strong foundation of mental clarity and focus, essential for advancing on their psychic development journey. The techniques outlined are not exhaustive but represent a comprehensive approach to preparing the mind for the profound work of exploring the psychic realm.

PHYSICAL WELLNESS AND PSYCHIC ABILITY

The intricate relationship between physical wellness and psychic ability is a subject of increasing interest within the realm of psychic development. Let's explore the significant impact of physical health on enhancing psychic sensitivity and capabilities, emphasizing the need for maintaining a balanced lifestyle to foster psychic growth.

The Interconnectedness of Physical and Mental Health

Physical and mental health are deeply interconnected, with each significantly influencing the other. Maintaining physical health is not only vital for overall well-being but also plays a crucial role in enhancing mental clarity and emotional stability, which are essential for psychic development. The synergy between physical and mental wellness creates a conducive environment for psychic abilities to flourish.

Exercise and Psychic Development

Regular physical activity is a cornerstone of good health, releasing endorphins that promote a sense of well-being, increase energy levels, and sharpen mental focus. Such a state of heightened mental clarity and emotional balance is conducive to psychic practices, enabling a clearer connection with one's intuitive senses. Activities such as yoga and tai chi, which integrate movement with mindful breathing and meditation, are particularly beneficial in harmonizing the body, mind, and spirit, thus enhancing psychic receptivity.

Nutrition and Energy Levels

Diet plays a significant role in physical and psychic health by influencing energy levels and cognitive function. Nutrient-rich foods, particularly those high in omega-3 fatty acids, antioxidants, and vitamins, can enhance brain function and, consequently, psychic sensitivity. A balanced diet supports not only physical health but also contributes to a clearer and more vibrant energy field, which is essential for psychic work.

Sleep and Psychic Integration

Quality sleep is fundamental to both physical health and psychic development. It provides an opportunity for the body to heal and rejuvenate, and for the mind to process and integrate psychic experiences. Dream work, an essential aspect of psychic development, benefits from restful sleep, as it is during this time that the subconscious mind is most receptive to psychic insights and messages.

Stress Management for Clearer Psychic Channels

Managing stress is crucial for maintaining physical health and clear psychic channels. High stress levels can cloud psychic perception and hinder the ability to connect with higher guidance. Techniques such as meditation, deep breathing exercises, and spending time in nature can help manage stress, thereby enhancing psychic sensitivity and protecting the energy field from negative influences.

The profound connection between physical wellness and psychic ability underscores the importance of a holistic approach to psychic development. By nurturing the body through exercise, nutrition, adequate rest, and stress management, individuals can create a strong foundation that supports the growth and refinement of psychic abilities. This integrated approach ensures that the journey of psychic development is both balanced and grounded in the well-being of the entire being.

Through diligent attention to physical health, individuals embarking on the psychic voyage can enhance their sensitivity, clarity, and connection to the unseen realm, unlocking their full psychic potential.

EMOTIONAL BALANCE

Emotional balance is essential for psychic development, as it allows for clearer perception and a stronger connection to intuitive insights. Let's delve into the importance of managing emotions and strategies to achieve emotional equilibrium, enhancing psychic abilities.

Understanding Emotional Influences

Emotions significantly impact psychic perception. Strong emotions, both positive and negative, can cloud judgment, distort messages from the spiritual realm, and interfere with the ability to connect deeply with one's inner self and the external psychic environment. Achieving emotional balance helps to clear these blockages, allowing for a more profound and clear psychic experience.

Techniques for Emotional Regulation

1. Mindfulness Meditation: Practicing mindfulness meditation helps in observing emotions without judgment, allowing one to understand their transient nature and reduce their overwhelming power. This practice aids in developing a calm and centered state of mind, conducive to psychic work.

2. Emotional Journaling: Writing down thoughts and feelings can provide an outlet for expressing emotions, leading to clarity and insights into personal emotional patterns. Recognizing these patterns is the

first step toward managing emotional reactions and maintaining psychic clarity.

3. Breathing Exercises: Deep breathing techniques are effective in calming the nervous system and reducing emotional intensity. Techniques such as the 4-7-8 breathing method can be particularly useful in moments of emotional upheaval, helping to restore balance and focus.

Enhancing Emotional Intelligence

Emotional intelligence plays a crucial role in managing emotions. It involves recognizing, understanding, and managing one's emotions and the emotions of others. Enhancing emotional intelligence through self-reflection, empathy practice, and communication skills can improve emotional regulation and psychic sensitivity.

The Role of Physical Exercise

Physical exercise is not only beneficial for physical health but also for emotional well-being. Activities such as yoga, tai chi, or even brisk walking can help release pent-up emotions, reduce stress, and increase overall emotional stability, creating a conducive environment for psychic development.

Establishing Healthy Boundaries

Setting healthy boundaries is essential for emotional balance, especially for individuals sensitive to the emotions of others. Learning to say no, prioritizing self-care, and distancing oneself from emotionally toxic situations can prevent emotional overwhelm and preserve psychic clarity.

The Importance of Emotional Healing

Addressing unresolved emotional issues is crucial for achieving emotional balance. Techniques such as therapy, energy healing, and forgiveness practices can facilitate emotional healing, releasing blockages that hinder psychic development and opening the pathway to a deeper connection with the psychic self.

Cultivating Positive Relationships

Surrounding oneself with supportive and understanding individuals can provide an emotional buffer against stress and negativity. Positive relationships encourage growth, provide comfort, and enhance the ability to maintain emotional balance amidst the challenges of psychic development.

Emotional balance is a cornerstone of psychic development. Managing emotions through mindfulness, emotional intelligence, physical exercise, healthy boundaries, emotional healing, and positive relationships can significantly enhance psychic perception. By achieving emotional equilibrium, individuals can ensure that their psychic journey is not hindered by emotional turbulence, leading to clearer insights and a deeper understanding of the psychic realm.

DEVELOPING
INTUITION

INTUITION: THE INNER VOICE

Cultivating intuition involves engaging in practices that enhance our innate ability to perceive and understand beyond the five senses. Let's explore various exercises and techniques designed to strengthen intuition, a key component of psychic development.

Daily Mindfulness and Journaling

The practice of mindfulness helps to cultivate a state of present awareness, which makes it easier to pick up on intuitive ideas. When it comes to tracking progress and trends in one's intuitive development, keeping a journal in which one records their experiences, feelings, and any intuitive hits that they receive during the day is a significant tool.

Enhancing Clairvoyance

It is possible to improve clairvoyance, also known as clear vision, by the practice of exercises that concentrate on the third eye chakra. These activities include visualizing the chakra opening, utilizing crystals such as fluorite or amethyst to promote psychic sight, and practicing meditation with the intention of improving visual intuition.

Psychic Protection

To keep oneself in a high vibrating state that is suitable to intuitive work, it is essential to have the ability to protect one's energy. Grounding exercises, picturing a white light of protection, and employing protective crystals are some of the techniques that can be utilized.

Practicing Psychometry

In order to receive intuitive signals, psychometry requires the practitioner to grasp an object and tune into the energy that it possesses. The ability to connect with the energy and history of one's physical objects is improved with the practice of this technique.

Telepathy and Symbol Recognition

Telepathy training can be a rewarding and enjoyable experience. This capacity can be strengthened by activities such as attempting to send or receive basic messages or photographs to a family member or acquaintance. Increasing one's intuitive understanding can also be accomplished by paying attention to symbols and signs that are present in everyday life and acquiescing to their interpretations.

Visualization and Future Tuning

The development of intuition can be greatly aided by engaging in activities such as practicing visualization and tuning into future events. The ability to acquire future insights can be improved by envisioning an event before it takes place and making a note of any intuitive impressions that result from this visualization.

Use of Divination Tools

Both tarot cards and oracle cards are extremely helpful tools for enhancing one's intuitive abilities. Deepening one's intuitive abilities can be accomplished by drawing daily cards and paying attention to the impressions and messages that they communicate without instantly inquiring about their significance.

Developing Clairsentience

Clairsentience, or clear feeling, allows individuals to receive intuitive information through feelings and sensations. Recognizing and trusting these feelings as valid forms of intuitive insight can enhance one's psychic sensitivity.

Keeping a High Vibration

Maintaining a high vibration through positive thoughts, high-vibrational foods, and joyful activities attracts similar energies and supports a strong intuitive connection.

Dream Journaling

A wealth of intuitive insight can be gleaned from one's dreams. Unlocking deeper levels of psychic awareness can be accomplished by keeping a dream journal in which one records and interprets one's psychic dreams.

By engaging in these practices, individuals can significantly enhance their intuitive abilities, leading to a deeper understanding of themselves and the world around them.

Each exercise not only develops specific psychic skills but also contributes to a holistic approach to psychic development, emphasizing the interconnectedness of mind, body, and spirit.

PRACTICES TO ENHANCE INTUITION

In the realm of psychic development, enhancing intuition is a pivotal aspect that can be cultivated through various practices and exercises. Let's delve into techniques designed to amplify intuitive abilities, providing a comprehensive guide to tapping into your inner psychic potential.

Eating High-Vibrational Foods: Incorporating foods that raise your energetic vibration, such as fresh fruits and organic dark chocolate, can enhance your aura and psychic abilities. A diet rich in high-vibrational foods not only supports physical well-being but also promotes a stronger connection to your psychic senses.

Telepathy and Clairvoyant Exercises: Engaging in exercises that stimulate mental telepathy and clairvoyance can be both fun and effective. Visualizing a friend and mentally requesting their contact or utilizing Zener cards to practice sending and receiving telepathic images are practical ways to develop these skills. These activities help in strengthening the psychic sight and the ability to communicate telepathically.

Activating the Third Eye: The third eye, located between the eyebrows, is considered the seat of intuition and psychic vision. Techniques such as gently tapping the third eye area and visualizing it opening can awaken clairvoyant abilities. Meditating with crystals like amethyst or lapis lazuli placed on the third eye can further enhance this process.

Dream Journaling: Dreams are a rich source of intuitive insight and clairvoyant messages. Keeping a dream journal facilitates the recognition of patterns or symbols that may emerge, offering valuable guidance and enhancing psychic sight.

Meditation and Solitude: Regular meditation and spending time alone are fundamental for clearing the mind and connecting with one's inner voice. These practices allow for a deeper exploration of the subconscious and can significantly boost intuition.

Connecting with Spirit Guides: Establishing a connection with spirit guides through meditation or rituals can open channels for receiving psychic information. Spirit guides offer wisdom and insight, assisting in the development of intuition and providing clarity on one's life path and purpose.

Rituals for Psychic Development: Engaging in rituals like smudging, using sacred objects, or chanting can create an energetic environment conducive to intuitive and psychic development. These practices help in setting intentions and opening up to higher knowledge.

Intuition Games and Exercises: Participating in games designed to train intuition, such as predicting who might call or choosing faster lines at stores, can sharpen intuitive abilities. Exercises like psychometry, where one reads the energy of objects, and practicing seeing auras are effective ways to enhance psychic perception.

Trusting and Acknowledging Intuition: Recognizing and

trusting gut reactions to people, places, and situations is crucial for psychic development. Keeping a journal to note these intuitive hits can reinforce the ability to rely on one's inner guidance.

Visualization Techniques: Visualization exercises, such as imagining detailed objects or scenarios, can improve clairvoyance and the connection with spirit guides. Practicing visualization helps in developing the mental imagery skills essential for psychic work.

Clearing Energy Blockages: Identifying and removing energy blockages is vital for a clear flow of psychic information. Visiting a healer or engaging in self-care practices that cleanse the aura can remove obstacles to psychic awareness.

Developing Psychic Abilities through Practice: Continuous practice of these techniques and exercises is key to unlocking one's psychic potential. Whether it's through meditation, connecting with spirit guides, or engaging in psychic exercises, regular practice enhances intuition and psychic abilities.

By integrating these practices into daily life, individuals can significantly enhance their intuition and psychic abilities, paving the way for a deeper understanding of themselves and the world around them.

INTUITION IN EVERYDAY LIFE

Integrating intuition into daily decision-making and relationships involves recognizing and acting upon the subtle, often non-verbal cues that guide us towards more authentic choices. Let's explore practical ways to apply intuition to enhance personal and professional life.

Intuition operates beyond conscious reasoning, relying on the brain's and body's ability to process information rapidly, based on accumulated knowledge and experiences. This instinctual guidance system aids in navigating ambiguity, making swift decisions, and recognizing the underlying truths in interactions with others and the environment.

Recognizing Intuitive Signals

Intuition manifests through bodily sensations and emotional responses, signaling alignment or misalignment with people, situations, or decisions. Positive intuitive feelings may include a sense of comfort, openness, and energy, indicating a conducive path or relationship. Conversely, feelings of discomfort, constriction, or drained energy can warn against certain choices or associations.

Developing Intuitive Decision-Making

To cultivate intuitive decision-making, focus on domain-specific improvement, enriching the knowledge base related to

your field or interests. Engage in practices that build critical thinking skills, such as scenario-based training and reflection on past decisions to refine your intuitive instincts. Trusting your gut in professional settings, especially when coupled with rational analysis, can lead to more effective and authentic decision-making.

Intuition and Relationships

Intuition plays a crucial role in forming and maintaining relationships. It helps discern underlying dynamics and compatibility, often before rational analysis can catch up. By paying attention to how you feel in someone's presence, you can gauge the potential for meaningful connection. Positive vibes, such as ease, openness, and mutual understanding, often indicate a healthy relationship, while negative vibes might suggest caution or reevaluation.

Practical Exercises to Enhance Intuition

1. Tune into your body: Regularly check in with your physical and emotional reactions to gauge your intuitive responses to people and situations.

2. Reflect on past decisions: Analyze decisions where you followed or ignored your intuition to understand the outcomes and sharpen your intuitive skills.

3. Practice mindfulness: Cultivate a habit of present-

moment awareness to enhance your sensitivity to intuitive signals.

4. Engage in intuitive games: Participate in activities designed to strengthen intuition, such as guessing games or using intuition apps.

Integrating intuition into everyday life enriches decision-making and relationships, grounding them in a deeper sense of knowing and authenticity. As you practice and trust your intuitive skills, you'll find yourself navigating life's complexities with greater ease and confidence, leading to more fulfilling outcomes both personally and professionally.

By embracing intuition as a complement to rational thought, we harness a powerful ally in the journey of life, enabling us to make choices that are aligned with our deepest values and truths.

ENERGY WORK

UNDERSTANDING ENERGY FIELDS: AURAS, CHAKRAS, AND ENERGY

Energy fields, auras, and chakras form the foundational elements of the psychic and spiritual aspects of our being, each playing a crucial role in our overall well-being. We will delve into their significance, functions, and the interconnectedness between them.

Auras and Their Layers

The aura is a luminous energy field surrounding every living being, reflecting the individual's emotional, physical, and spiritual state. It comprises several layers, each vibrating at a unique frequency and representing different aspects of our existence:

- The Etheric Body, closest to the physical body, mirrors our health and vitality.

- The Emotional Body changes with our feelings, illustrating our emotional landscape.

- The Mental Body embodies our thoughts and intellectual processes.

- The Astral Body connects to higher emotions and spiritual experiences.
- The Causal Body, or the etheric template, relates to our soul purpose and spiritual path.

These layers collectively offer insights into our holistic well-being, allowing us to identify areas of strength or imbalance.

Chakras: The Energy Centers

Chakras are vital energy centers within our body, each corresponding to significant aspects of our physical, emotional, and spiritual health. They include:

- The Root Chakra influences our sense of security and grounding.
- The Sacral Chakra affects our creativity and sexual energy.
- The Solar Plexus Chakra governs our personal power and self-esteem.
- The Heart Chakra is central to our capacity for love and compassion.
- The Throat Chakra impacts our communication and expression.
- The Third Eye Chakra

relates to intuition and insight.

- The Crown Chakra connects us to the divine and universal consciousness.

Balancing these chakras ensures the optimal flow of energy through our body, enhancing our physical, emotional, and spiritual well-being.

The Connection Between Auras and Chakras

The aura and chakras are deeply interconnected, with each chakra influencing specific layers of the aura. This connection highlights the complex interplay between our physical body and the energy field surrounding it. For instance, imbalances in a chakra can manifest as disturbances in the corresponding aura layer, affecting our emotional and physical health.

Understanding and nurturing this connection through practices such as meditation, aura cleansing, and chakra balancing can lead to enhanced well-being, spiritual growth, and a harmonious balance between mind, body, and spirit.

Practical Applications

To maintain a vibrant and balanced energy field, consider incorporating the following practices into your daily routine:

- Aura Cleansing: Techniques such as smudging with sage, taking salt baths, and visualization can help clear the aura of negative energy.

- Chakra Balancing: Meditation, sound healing, and yoga can align and harmonize the chakras, promoting the free flow of energy.

- Mindful Awareness: Regularly tuning into your body and emotions can help you become more aware of the state of your chakras and aura, guiding you to practices that restore balance and vitality.

By understanding and working with our energy fields, auras, and chakras, we can unlock deeper levels of healing, self-awareness, and spiritual growth, fostering a life of harmony, health, and fulfillment.

ENERGY HEALING TECHNIQUES

Energy healing is a profound practice that taps into the body's intrinsic ability to restore balance and harmony. Central to this concept is the understanding that every individual possesses a unique energy field, which can become unbalanced due to various factors including stress, illness, and emotional turmoil. Let's delve into the basics of energy healing, offering readers practical techniques for self-care and the promotion of inner wellness.

Understanding the Principles of Energy Healing

At the heart of energy healing lies the principle that the body is more than just a physical entity; it is a complex system of energy fields interacting within and without. These fields, often referred to as the aura or the subtle bodies, encompass the physical, emotional, mental, and spiritual aspects of our being. Energy healing works by influencing these fields, aiming to clear blockages and restore equilibrium, thereby facilitating the body's natural healing processes.

Techniques for Self-Energy Healing

1. Grounding: Grounding is the foundational step in any energy healing practice. It involves connecting with the earth's energy to stabilize your own energy field. Techniques include walking barefoot on grass,

visualizing roots extending from your feet into the earth, or simply sitting and focusing on your connection to the ground beneath you.

2. Centering: Centering is the process of aligning your spiritual, physical, and emotional centers. Practice by focusing on your breath, visualizing it moving through the center of your body, anchoring you firmly in your own being.

3. Cleansing Your Aura: Your aura can accumulate negative energy. Techniques for cleansing include visualizing a shower of light washing over you, gently sweeping your body with your hands to brush away unwanted energies, or using sage smoke or sound vibrations from bells or singing bowls.

4. Chakra Balancing: The chakras are vital energy centers in your body, each associated with different aspects of your physical and emotional life. Balancing them involves focusing on each chakra, from the root to the crown, and visualizing them spinning in harmony, often accompanied by specific colors or sounds.

5. Reiki: Reiki is a Japanese technique for stress reduction and relaxation that also promotes healing. It's based on the idea that an unseen "life force energy" flows through us. Practitioners can learn to channel energy into someone by means of touch, to activate the natural healing processes of the patient's body and restore physical and emotional well-being.

6. Pranic Healing: Pranic healing is a practice that utilizes the body's life force to heal the body's energy. This technique involves scanning the body for depleted or congested areas and cleansing these areas with fresh prana (energy) and thereby revitalizing the body.

Incorporating Energy Healing into Daily Life

Energy healing techniques can be seamlessly integrated into your daily routine. Begin or end your day with grounding and centering exercises to maintain balance. Cleanse your aura after a stressful day or when feeling emotionally overwhelmed. Chakra balancing can be done weekly to maintain energy flow, and simple Reiki techniques can be self-applied to address specific ailments or emotional states.

Enhancing Your Practice

To enhance your energy healing practice, consider incorporating meditation, yoga, or tai chi, which support energy flow and provide additional grounding and centering benefits. Keeping a journal to note your experiences, feelings, and any changes you observe can be incredibly insightful.

Energy healing is a deeply personal journey and what works for one may not work for another. Experiment with different techniques to find what resonates best with you. Remember, the goal of energy healing is not just to heal the body but to create a harmonious balance within your entire being, leading to a more peaceful, healthy, and fulfilling life.

PROTECTING AND CLEANSING YOUR ENERGY

Psychic protection and energy cleansing are crucial practices for anyone delving into psychic development. These techniques safeguard your spiritual, emotional, and mental wellbeing, helping to maintain a vibrant aura and emotional balance. Let's explore a variety of methods to shield and cleanse your energy, ensuring you remain grounded and protected on your psychic voyage.

Visualization Techniques for Protection

Visualization is a powerful tool for psychic protection. Envisioning a shield of white light surrounding your body can block negative energy and psychic attacks. You can also imagine yourself within a sphere of bright white light or surrounded by a cloak of darkness for protection. Regular practice of these visualizations strengthens your auric shield, providing a robust barrier against external negativity.

Salt for Spiritual Cleansing and Protection

Salt is renowned for its negative energy-absorbing properties, making it an effective element in psychic cleansing and protection rituals. Adding sea salt to bathwater can create a purifying soak, helping to neutralize negativity from your aura.

Sprinkling salt in your living space or around yourself can also create a protective barrier against harmful energies.

Crystals for Psychic Protection

Crystals are valuable allies in shielding against negative energies. Placing protective stones like smoky quartz, jasper, or kyanite around your home or wearing them as jewelry can fortify your psychic defense. These crystals can also be placed around the chakras or used to make a protective elixir.

Smudging for Energy Cleansing

Smudging with sage or other herbs is a traditional practice for cleansing spaces and auras of negative energy. This ritual can help create a protective barrier around you, fostering a safe and sacred environment. Smudging can also assist with grounding and stability, fortifying your defenses against psychic attacks.

Grounding and Centering Practices

Establishing a strong energetic foundation through grounding and centering is essential for psychic protection. Techniques include visualizing roots extending from your feet into the earth, focusing on your breath, and engaging in physical activities that connect you with nature. Grounding helps discharge unwanted energy and stabilizes your aura.

Psychic Shielding Strategies

Creating a psychic shield involves envisioning a barrier around you that blocks negative influences. This shield can be imagined as a wall of energy, a glass sphere, or a circle of white light. Finding a personal symbol that represents safety and security can enhance the effectiveness of your shield.

The Role of Positive Mindset and Self-Care

Maintaining a positive mindset and practicing self-care are foundational aspects of psychic protection. Focusing on gratitude, engaging in activities that bring joy, and taking time for relaxation can raise your vibration, strengthening your aura and making you less susceptible to energy drains.

Discernment and Spiritual Energy Maintenance

Learning to discern between positive and negative entities and consciously choosing to connect only with those of light is crucial for psychic safety. Strengthening your spiritual  energy through practices like Reiki, meditation, and energy cleansing rituals ensures your psychic defenses remain robust.

Empathic Protection Techniques

For empaths and clairsentients, differentiating between personal emotions and those absorbed from others is vital. A simple but effective technique involves stating, "If this is not mine, please take it away," to release unwelcome energies.

By incorporating these practices into your daily routine, you can navigate your psychic development journey with confidence, ensuring your energy remains clear, balanced, and protected.

PSYCHIC TOOLS
AND TECHNIQUES

TAROT AND ORACLE CARDS

Tarot and Oracle cards serve as powerful tools for gaining insights into one's life, providing guidance, and facilitating personal growth. While Tarot cards follow a structured system with a fixed number of cards divided into Major and Minor Arcana, Oracle cards are more free-form, offering a variety of themes and messages without a set structure.

Integrating Tarot and Oracle Cards

Combining Tarot and Oracle cards in readings can deepen your understanding and provide clearer guidance. Begin by setting your intention for the reading and cleansing your deck. This preparation helps in aligning your energy with the cards and clarifies the purpose of the reading. When faced with ambiguous messages from the Tarot, Oracle cards can offer clarification, adding layers of meaning to the reading. For example, drawing an Ace of Pentacles in a Tarot reading suggests new beginnings in financial matters, while an Oracle card can further clarify the nature of these opportunities.

Practical Steps for a Combined Reading

1. Shuffle the Decks: Shuffle both the Tarot and Oracle decks while focusing on your question. This integrates their energies, preparing them for the reading.

2. Ask Your Question: Clearly articulate the question you

seek to answer. Specific questions lead to more focused insights.

3. Draw the Cards: Select cards from both decks. For a daily overview, four cards can provide a comprehensive guide.

4. Interpret the Message: Analyze the symbolism and messages of both card types. Combining the structured insight of Tarot with the intuitive guidance of Oracle cards offers a more rounded perspective.

Tips for Accurate Readings

- Pay Attention to Imagery: The artwork and symbols on the cards are potent sources of insight. They can trigger intuitive hits and reveal underlying themes or advice.

- Retain a Sense of Wonder: Approach readings with openness and curiosity. A relaxed mindset enhances intuition and the accuracy of the insights gained.

- Avoid Overuse: To maintain the accuracy of the readings, give adequate space between sessions. This allows insights to manifest and prevents clouding your intuition with repetitive queries.

Choosing Your Decks

Selecting decks that resonate with you is crucial. The theme and artwork of the Oracle deck should align with your personal beliefs and interests, as this strengthens your intuitive connection with the cards. Whether drawn to the symbolism of animals, angels, or other spiritual themes, choose a deck that speaks to you on a personal level.

Incorporating Oracle Cards for Personal Growth

Oracle cards are not just tools for divination but also for self-reflection and personal growth. Asking empowering questions, focusing on your intentions, and trusting your instincts during readings can significantly enhance your psychic and intuitive abilities.

By integrating Tarot and Oracle cards, you tap into a synergistic method of divination that combines the structured guidance of Tarot with the flexible, intuitive insights of Oracle cards. This approach enriches readings, offering deeper understanding and clarity on your psychic voyage.

PENDULUMS AND DOWSING

Pendulums and dowsing are ancient practices used for psychic development, divination, and the search for hidden objects or resources. Let's delve into the mystical world of pendulums and dowsing rods, tools that have been used by psychics, dowsers, and healers throughout history to tap into intuitive insights and energies beyond the physical realm.

Understanding Pendulums

A pendulum is a weighted object suspended from a string or chain, used to gain insights through its movements in response to questions or as a guide in energy work. The key to working with a pendulum lies in its simplicity and the psychic connection established between the tool and its user. The pendulum acts as an amplifier for the subtle energies and inner knowledge of the practitioner, translating intuitive signals into physical movements.

Selecting a pendulum is a personal journey; it should feel right in your hands and resonate with your energy. Materials vary from crystals, which are popular due to their energetic properties, to metal, wood, or glass. Each material and shape can offer different sensations or affinities, emphasizing the importance of choosing one that aligns with your psychic development goals.

Using a Pendulum

To begin, hold the pendulum between your thumb and forefinger, steadying your elbow on a flat surface to minimize involuntary movements. Start by asking simple yes/no questions to establish the pendulum's direction for each type of response. Commonly, forward and backward movements indicate "yes," while side to side suggests "no." However, these responses can vary and should be personally established.

The practice involves centering oneself, reaching a state of calm and focus, to ensure that the pendulum's movements are guided by higher consciousness rather than conscious thoughts or physical tremors. Regular meditation and grounding exercises can enhance your connection to the pendulum, refining the accuracy and depth of the insights received.

Dowsing Basics

Dowsing extends beyond pendulum use, often involving rods or sticks to locate water, minerals, or other objects. The principle, however, remains the same: it is a practice that taps into the user's subconscious knowledge and the energies of the earth. Dowsing rods, typically L-shaped or Y-shaped, are held loosely in the hands and move in response to the presence of the sought-after material or energy.

Like pendulum dowsing, ethical considerations are paramount. It is advised to dowse with clear intentions, seeking permission from the universal consciousness and respecting the privacy and free will of others when asking questions or searching for information.

Applications in Psychic Development

Pendulums and dowsing rods can be invaluable tools for psychic development, offering a tangible way to connect with intuitive insights, guide energy healing practices, and make decisions aligned with one's highest good. They can be used for chakra balancing, identifying energy blockages, and enhancing meditation practices by providing feedback and focus.

Furthermore, these tools can foster a deeper sense of trust in one's intuitive abilities, encouraging a more open and receptive state of mind. As you work with a pendulum or dowsing rods, you become more attuned to subtle energies, which can enhance your psychic abilities and spiritual growth.

Practical Tips for Success

- Cleanse your pendulum or dowsing rods regularly to clear accumulated energies.
- Practice regularly, but don't over-rely on your tools; use them as aids rather than crutches.
- Record your sessions to track progress, patterns, and insights gained.
- Trust the process, but also apply discernment; not all answers are literal or immediately clear.

The art of pendulum dowsing and dowsing with rods offers a profound way to explore the unseen, develop psychic abilities, and navigate the spiritual journey with confidence and clarity.

By understanding and respecting these tools, you open yourself to deeper insights and connections with the energies that permeate our world.

CRYSTALS AND PSYCHIC DEVELOPMENT

Crystals have been revered across cultures for centuries, not only for their beauty but for their profound psychic and energetic properties. Let's investigate how these natural treasures can amplify and refine one's psychic development, providing practical advice on harnessing their power.

The Essence of Crystals in Psychic Work

Crystals operate at vibrational frequencies that can resonate with human energy fields, enhancing psychic abilities such as intuition, clairvoyance, and energy healing. Each crystal, with its unique structure, offers distinct benefits—ranging from grounding and protection to amplifying psychic communications. Their energies can help in attuning to the spiritual realm, facilitating a clearer channel for psychic insights and messages.

Selecting Your Crystals

When embarking on psychic development with crystals, the first step is selection. Intuition plays a key role here; you are likely to be drawn to crystals that match your vibrational needs. Some of the most potent crystals for psychic enhancement include:

- Amethyst: Enhances intuition and spiritual awareness, promotes calmness and clarity.

- Quartz Crystal: Amplifies energy, thoughts, and the effects of other crystals. It's a master healer.

- Labradorite: Acts as a protective ally, deflecting unwanted energies, and facilitating safe exploration of alternative levels of consciousness.

- Lapis Lazuli: Opens the third eye chakra, enhancing psychic vision and facilitating spiritual journeying.

- Moonstone: Promotes intuition and empathy, offering protection during travel on land and at sea.

Cleansing and Charging Your Crystals

Before use, it's essential to cleanse new crystals to clear them of previous energies. This can be done through various methods such as smudging with sage, burying in the earth, or soaking in moonlight. Charging your crystals under the full moon replenishes their energy, ensuring they operate at their highest vibrational capacity.

Integrating Crystals into Psychic Practices

To incorporate crystals into your psychic development:

- Meditation: Holding a crystal or placing it on relevant chakras during meditation can deepen your practice, enhance psychic visions, and promote spiritual guidance.

- Energy Healing: Crystals can be used to balance and activate the chakras, facilitating healing and enhancing psychic sensitivity.

- Psychic Readings: Placing crystals near your workspace can create a protective and clarifying energy, sharpening psychic insights and grounding both the reader and querent.

Forming a Bond with Your Crystals

Developing a personal relationship with your crystals is vital. Spend time with them, attuning to their energies and allowing their vibrations to align with yours. This bond not only enhances their effectiveness in psychic work but also turns them into powerful allies on your spiritual journey.

Ethical Considerations

While crystals are powerful tools, they should be used with respect and intention. Remember, they are not a substitute for personal work and growth. Instead, they serve as aids in amplifying your innate psychic abilities and spiritual connections.

Advanced Techniques

For those looking to deepen their practice:

- Crystal Grids: Arranging crystals in specific geometric formations can create powerful energy vortexes, enhancing psychic abilities and facilitating communication with the spiritual realm.

- Dream Work: Placing specific crystals under your pillow or by your bedside can promote lucid dreaming and astral travel, offering profound psychic insights.

Crystals offer a tangible connection to the vibrational world, serving as tools and companions in the exploration of psychic abilities. By understanding their properties, respecting their energies, and integrating them into your practice, you can significantly enhance your psychic development journey.

PSYCHIC
COMMUNICATION

MEDIUMSHIP BASICS - BRIDGING THE WORLDS

Mediumship stands as a profound psychic discipline, enabling communication between the physical world and the spirit realm. Let's introduce the foundational aspects of developing mediumship abilities, guiding readers through the initial steps towards becoming a medium.

Understanding Mediumship

Mediumship is the practice of mediating communication between spirits of the deceased and living humans. Mediums use their psychic abilities to sense, see, hear, and relay messages from the spirit world. This process requires a deep level of psychic sensitivity and an open, receptive state of consciousness.

Types of Mediumship

Mediumship manifests in various forms, each with unique characteristics:

- Mental Mediumship: The medium receives messages mentally, through clairvoyance (seeing), clairsentience (feeling), and clairaudience (hearing).
- Physical Mediumship: Involves physical phenomena,

such as objects moving or unexplained sounds, produced by spirits to communicate.

- Trance Mediumship: The medium enters a trance state, allowing spirits to speak directly through them.

Developing Your Abilities

Mediumship development begins with understanding and enhancing your psychic foundation. Key practices include:

- Meditation: Regular meditation enhances psychic sensitivity and mental clarity, vital for connecting with the spirit world.

- Energy Work: Learning to manage and protect your energy field is crucial for safe mediumship practice. Techniques such as grounding, centering, and shielding are foundational.

- Psychic Development Exercises: Engaging in exercises to develop your clair senses (clairvoyance, clairsentience, clairaudience, claircognizance) prepares you for receiving spirit communications.

Connecting with Spirit Guides

Spirit guides are entities that assist individuals in their spiritual journey. Establishing a connection with your spirit guides is a critical step in mediumship. They can offer protection, guidance, and facilitate communication with other spirits. Meditation, intention-setting, and asking for signs are ways to foster this connection.

Ethical Considerations

Mediumship carries significant responsibility. Ethical practices include:

- Consent: Always obtain consent from both the spirit and the person receiving the message.

- Integrity: Share messages truthfully and compassionately, without altering them to suit expectations.

- Confidentiality: Respect the privacy of the messages and the individuals involved.

Starting Your Practice

- Join a Development Circle: These groups offer a supportive environment for practicing mediumship under guidance.

- Practice Readings: Begin with friends or family open to receiving messages. Focus on delivering messages with integrity and compassion.

- Trust Your Intuition: Trusting the information you receive is crucial. Doubt can hinder your ability to interpret messages accurately.

Challenges and Overcoming Them

Mediumship development can be challenging, with common hurdles including fear, doubt, and interpreting messages.

Overcoming these challenges involves practice, trust in your abilities, and support from mentors or development circles.

Continuing Your Journey

Mediumship is a lifelong journey of learning and growth. Continuing to develop your psychic abilities, deepening your connection with spirit guides, and adhering to ethical practices are ongoing aspects of being a medium.

SPIRIT GUIDES AND HOW TO CONNECT

Spirit guides are non-physical entities that assist us in navigating the journey of our lives, offering guidance, wisdom, and support from the spiritual realm. Let's explore the nature of spirit guides and outlines practical steps for connecting with them to enhance psychic development.

Nature of Spirit Guides

Spirit guides come in many forms, reflecting the diversity of the spiritual realm. They may present themselves as ancestors, animals, light beings, or even figures from historical or mythological contexts. Regardless of their form, their purpose is universal: to provide guidance, support, and insight as we navigate our spiritual and earthly paths.

Recognizing Your Spirit Guides

Identifying your spirit guides begins with the acknowledgment of their presence. Many people have experienced moments of intuition, comfort, or guidance that seem to come from beyond themselves. These moments can often be attributed to the subtle influence of spirit guides.

Communicating with Your Spirit Guides

The process of connecting with your spirit guides is deeply personal and can be developed through various practices:

- Meditation: Meditation creates a quiet space for your mind, making it easier to sense and communicate with your guides. Begin with the intention to connect, inviting your spirit guides to reveal themselves in a way that is for your highest good.

- Dream Work: Pay attention to your dreams, as spirit guides often communicate through this accessible subconscious state. Keeping a dream journal can help discern messages and symbols from your guides.

- Nature Walks: Spirit guides can use the natural world to send messages. Time spent in nature can facilitate a deeper connection, allowing for a clearer communication channel.

- Automatic Writing: This involves writing without conscious thought, allowing your spirit guides to communicate through the written word. It requires a state of relaxation and openness to the flow of information from your guides.

Building a Relationship

Connecting with your spirit guides is akin to developing a friendship. It requires time, openness, and patience. Regularly engaging in practices that promote connection can strengthen this relationship. Express gratitude for their guidance and support, acknowledging their presence in your life.

Signs and Symbols

Spirit guides communicate through signs and symbols, which can be personal and unique to each individual. Common signs include repeating numbers, feathers in unexpected places, or specific animals repeatedly crossing your path. Learning to recognize and interpret these signs is a crucial aspect of developing your psychic abilities.

Trust and Intuition

A key element in connecting with your spirit guides is trust —trust in the existence of guides, in their benevolent purpose, and in your ability to communicate with them. Developing your intuition plays a significant role in this process, as it is often through intuitive feelings, thoughts, or impressions that guides communicate.

Ethical Considerations

It's important to approach communication with spirit guides with respect and integrity. Set boundaries for the type of guidance you seek and be discerning about the messages received. Ensure that the guidance aligns with your highest good and ethical standards.

Practice and Patience

Like any skill, connecting with spirit guides improves with

practice. Regularly engaging in meditation, dream analysis, and other connecting practices will enhance your ability to communicate with your guides. Patience is crucial, as this connection may develop gradually.

Spirit guides are invaluable allies in our psychic development journey, offering guidance, support, and insight. By cultivating a relationship with your guides through meditation, nature, and other practices, you open yourself to a deeper understanding of the spiritual realm and your place within it. Trust, patience, and openness are key to developing this profound connection.

INTERPRETING MESSAGES FROM THE OTHER SIDE

Understanding and interpreting messages from the spirit world is a nuanced art, blending intuition with a deep awareness of the symbolic language used by spirits. Let's explore the realm of spiritual communication, offering insights into deciphering the signs and symbols conveyed by the other side.

The Language of the Spirit World

The spirit world communicates through a symbolic language, transcending words to convey messages through feelings, images, signs, and synchronicities. These communications can appear in dreams, during meditations, or in everyday life, often when least expected.

Recognizing Signs and Symbols

The first step in interpreting messages from the spirit world is to recognize when a sign or symbol is presented. Common forms include:

- Repeating Numbers: Sequences like 111, 333, or 1212 often appear to convey specific guidance or reassurance from the spirit realm.

- Animals and Insects: Encounters with animals or

insects, especially in unusual circumstances, can be messengers carrying important spiritual insights.

· Objects: Finding objects in unexpected places, such as feathers or coins, can be signs from the spirit world, symbolizing comfort, presence, or messages from loved ones.

Dream Interpretation

Dreams are a powerful medium for receiving messages from the other side. Spirits often communicate through dreams as our subconscious minds are more open to receiving spiritual messages. Keeping a dream journal can help in recognizing patterns, symbols, and recurring themes that may hold significant messages.

Intuition and Inner Knowing

Intuition plays a critical role in interpreting messages from the spirit world. It is the inner knowing or gut feeling that often guides the understanding of a message's relevance or meaning. Trusting your intuition and allowing it to guide the interpretation process is crucial.

Synchronicities

Synchronicities are meaningful coincidences that occur in our lives, often seen as signs from the universe or spirit guides. Recognizing and interpreting these synchronicities requires attentiveness to the flow of life and an openness to receiving messages.

Symbolic Interpretation

The interpretation of symbols is highly personal and can vary significantly from one person to another. Context, personal associations, and cultural meanings all play a part in deciphering the messages conveyed through symbols. Meditation and reflection can aid in understanding the personal relevance of a symbol.

Developing a Practice

Developing a consistent practice for receiving and interpreting messages can enhance one's ability to communicate with the spirit world. Practices might include:

- Meditation: Creating space for quiet reflection and openness to receiving messages.
- Journaling: Recording signs, symbols, and intuitive insights to track patterns and messages over time.
- Learning: Studying the symbolic meanings of animals, numbers, and other common symbols can provide a foundation for interpretation.

Challenges in Interpretation

Interpreting messages from the spirit world is not always straightforward. Misinterpretation can occur, especially when desires or fears cloud judgment. Approaching interpretation with a clear mind and an open heart, seeking clarity rather than validation, can mitigate these challenges.

Interpreting messages from the spirit world is a deeply personal and evolving practice. It requires patience, openness, and a willingness to explore the depths of symbolic language. By honing our intuitive abilities and paying attention to the signs and symbols that surround us, we can develop a richer, more meaningful connection with the spiritual realm, enhancing our psychic development journey.

Sensation of
- Astral Projection, Remote Viewing
Retrocognition Experience and Past-Life Regression

ADVANCED PSYCHIC
PRACTICES

ASTRAL PROJECTION AND REMOTE VIEWING

Astral projection and remote viewing are advanced psychic practices that allow individuals to experience and explore beyond the limits of the physical body and the immediate environment. Let's delve into the techniques, purposes, and ethical considerations of these profound practices, offering a guide for those seeking to expand their psychic journey into new dimensions.

Astral Projection

Astral projection, also known as an out-of-body experience (OBE), is the practice of consciously separating the astral body (spirit or consciousness) from the physical body to travel in the astral plane. This plane is a dimension of reality beyond the physical, populated with entities, spirits, and other travelers.

Techniques for Astral Projection

1. Relaxation: Achieving a deep state of relaxation is crucial. This can be done through meditation, deep breathing, or progressive muscle relaxation techniques.

2. Concentration: Focusing your mind on a single point

or intent. Visualization techniques, such as imagining yourself floating out of your body or visualizing a rope you can climb out with, can be effective.

3. Separation: Sensing the moment of separation between the astral and physical bodies. This may feel like floating, flying, or suddenly finding oneself in a different location.

Remote Viewing

Remote viewing is a form of psychic clairvoyance where individuals can perceive information about a distant or unseen target, including locations, objects, or people. It involves accessing the universal mind or collective consciousness to gather information beyond the constraints of time and space.

Techniques for Remote Viewing

1. Target Selection: Begin with a specific target in mind. The target should be something unknown to the viewer to avoid preconceived ideas or biases.

2. Quiet Mind: Achieve a state of mental stillness through meditation or relaxation techniques to reduce the noise of everyday thoughts and enhance psychic receptivity.

3. Receiving Information: Allow impressions, images,

feelings, and thoughts about the target to come to you without judgment or analysis.

4. Recording Impressions: Documenting the received information as precisely as possible, without attempting to interpret or rationalize it during the viewing session.

Purposes and Benefits

Both astral projection and remote viewing offer profound opportunities for personal and spiritual growth. They can enhance one's understanding of the self and the universe, facilitate healing, provide insight into past or future events, and offer experiences of profound connection and oneness with all existence.

Ethical Considerations

When engaging in astral projection and remote viewing, ethical considerations must be taken into account. Respect for the privacy and autonomy of others is paramount. These abilities should be used for positive purposes, such as personal growth, healing, and the greater good, rather than for harm or unwarranted intrusion.

Challenges and Overcoming Them

Practitioners may encounter fear, disbelief, or difficulty in achieving or controlling experiences. Overcoming these challenges involves practice, patience, and the development of a supportive community or guidance from experienced practitioners. Grounding and protective techniques are also essential to ensure safety and well-being.

Astral projection and remote viewing represent gateways to the unseen realms, offering unique insights and experiences beyond the physical world. With dedicated practice, ethical engagement, and an open heart, these practices can unveil the mysteries of existence and deepen one's psychic voyage.

PAST LIFE REGRESSION

Past life regression is a fascinating journey into the depths of the soul's history, offering insights into our spiritual journey across lifetimes. Let's explore the techniques and insights gained from past life regression, illuminating how these glimpses into our past selves can influence our current path and spiritual growth.

Understanding Past Life Regression

Past life regression is a therapeutic practice that uses hypnosis or meditation to guide individuals back through time to explore memories and experiences from previous lifetimes. This exploration is rooted in the belief in reincarnation, the concept that the soul experiences multiple lifetimes for learning, growth, and evolution.

Techniques for Past Life Regression

The most common method for past life regression is hypnotic regression, where a trained therapist guides the individual into a deeply relaxed state. Once in this state, the individual can access memories from past lives, often triggered by the therapist's questions or prompts.

- Self-Guided Meditation: For those seeking a more personal exploration, self-guided meditation techniques can also facilitate access to past life memories. Focusing on intentions and using visualization can help unlock the doors to past experiences.

- Group Regression Sessions: Conducted by a facilitator, these sessions guide a group of individuals through a collective regression experience, often leading to profound insights and shared experiences.

- Symbolic Resonance: Utilizing symbols, objects, or locations that resonate on a deep, intuitive level can also serve as portals to past life memories, helping individuals connect with specific time periods or experiences.

Gaining Insights from Past Lives

Past life regression can uncover patterns, relationships, and unresolved issues that have carried over into the current lifetime, offering explanations for certain behaviors, phobias, or affinities.

- Healing and Resolution: Understanding past traumas and relationships can bring healing and closure, allowing individuals to resolve past issues and move forward with greater clarity and purpose.

- Soul Lessons: Insights into the challenges and lessons of past lives can illuminate the soul's journey and purpose, enhancing spiritual growth and development.

- Karmic Relationships: Recognizing

souls from past lives in current relationships can deepen understanding and foster forgiveness, compassion, and love.

Ethical Considerations and Safety

Past life regression should be approached with respect and care, ensuring that it is conducted in a safe and supportive environment. It is crucial to work with a qualified therapist who can navigate the complex emotions and experiences that may arise.

Challenges and Overcoming Them

Some individuals may find it difficult to access past life memories or may encounter distressing or confusing experiences. It's important to maintain an open mind and heart, allowing the regression to unfold naturally. Support from the therapist, along with grounding and protective practices, can help manage any challenges that arise.

Past life regression offers a unique window into the soul's eternal journey, providing valuable insights into our spiritual evolution and the lessons we are here to learn. By exploring the narratives of our past selves, we can gain a deeper understanding of our current life's purpose, challenges, and opportunities for growth. This journey into the past enriches our psychic development, enhancing our connection to the unseen realm and our understanding of the timeless nature of our existence.

DREAM WORK

Dream work is an integral part of psychic development, offering a window into the subconscious mind and a pathway to intuitive insights. It encompasses interpreting psychic dreams, engaging in lucid dreaming, and harnessing dream messages for personal growth. Dreams are not just random neural firings in the brain; they can be psychic experiences filled with symbolism, messages from the spirit realm, or previews of potential futures.

Interpreting Psychic Dreams

Psychic dreams are more vivid, symbolic, and sometimes prophetic than ordinary dreams. They often contain significant messages or insights about personal development, life events, or spiritual guidance. To interpret psychic dreams, start by keeping a dream journal. Record everything you can recall upon waking, noting the emotions, colors, symbols, and characters present. Over time, patterns will emerge, helping to decode the symbolic language of your subconscious.

Symbols in dreams can be personal or universal. For example, water often symbolizes emotions, while flying might represent freedom or the desire to escape. However, the interpretation of these symbols can vary based on personal experiences and feelings. Reflecting on how these symbols relate to your life can provide clarity and insight.

Understanding the Dream State

Dreams occur in various sleep stages, notably REM (Rapid Eye Movement) sleep, characterized by intense brain activity, vivid dreams, and a hybrid state of consciousness blending wakefulness and dreaming. Psychological aspects of dreaming reveal a close relationship between dream content and emotional well-being, where lucid dreams—those in which the dreamer is aware they are dreaming—offer avenues for emotional exploration and mental health management.

Engaging in Lucid Dreaming

Lucid dreaming is the practice of becoming conscious within your dream, realizing you are dreaming as the dream unfolds. This awareness can sometimes allow you to control the dream's narrative, offering unique opportunities for exploration and insight. To induce lucid dreaming, try reality checks throughout the day—like reading text or checking a clock, as these actions can behave oddly in dreams. Techniques such as the Wake Back to Bed (WBTB) method, where you wake up after five to six hours of sleep and then go back to sleep intending to become lucid, can also be effective.

In the context of psychic development, lucid dreaming can be a powerful tool for self-exploration and accessing deeper layers of the subconscious. It can be used to practice psychic skills, meet with spirit guides, or work through personal obstacles in a safe and malleable environment.

Techniques for Achieving Lucid Dreaming

1. Reality Testing: A practice involving periodic checks throughout the day to discern whether you're dreaming, fostering a habit that transitions into the dream state.

2. Mnemonic Induction of Lucid Dreams (MILD): Invokes a strong intention to remember that you're dreaming, often coupled with visualization of becoming lucid in a recent dream.

3. Wake Back to Bed (WBTB): Waking after 5-6 hours of sleep, then staying awake briefly before going back to sleep to increase the chances of entering REM sleep and achieving lucidity.

4. Wake-Initiated Lucid Dream (WILD): Entering a dream state directly from wakefulness while maintaining consciousness, a technique that requires recognizing the hypnagogic state without falling into unconsciousness.

Additional methods include the Finger-Induced Lucid Dream (FILD), where finger movements aim to keep the prefrontal cortex awake, and the Modified Castaneda Technique, based on intense focus on one's hands before sleep, reinforcing the notion of dreaming awareness. The Wake-Initiated Lucid Dream (WILD) technique focuses on the hypnagogic state to transition into a lucid dream.

Enhancing Lucid Dreaming

Practices for enhancing lucid dreaming include maintaining proper sleep hygiene and exploring supplements or devices designed to promote awareness within dreams. Consistent sleep schedules and a conducive sleep environment support uninterrupted sleep, crucial for dream recall and lucidity. Some individuals may also experiment with supplements or technological aids, such as masks emitting light patterns or smartphone apps playing auditory cues during REM sleep, to signal the dream state without waking.

Applications and Therapeutic Uses

Lucid dreaming holds significant therapeutic potential, particularly in addressing nightmares and anxiety-related sleep disturbances. It enables individuals to confront fears in a controlled, safe dream environment, offering a unique space for engaging with the subconscious. Beyond therapy, lucid dreaming serves as a powerful tool for creativity and problem-solving, allowing for uninhibited exploration of ideas beyond the constraints of reality.

Challenges and Considerations

While lucid dreaming offers profound insights and opportunities for personal development, it also presents challenges, such as the potential for vivid nightmares or the exacerbation of certain sleep disorders. Awareness of these risks, coupled with responsible practice and attention to one's mental and emotional well-being, is essential for safely navigating the complexities of lucid dreaming.

Harnessing Dream Messages for Personal Growth

Dreams can offer guidance, highlight areas of your life that need attention, and even suggest solutions to problems. To harness these messages:

- Pay attention to recurring dreams or themes, as they often highlight unresolved issues or important messages from your subconscious.

- Look for solutions or guidance within the dream. Even if the message seems cryptic, it may offer insight into your waking life challenges.

- Use dreams as a tool for personal reflection. Consider how the emotions, scenarios, and symbols in your dreams relate to your inner thoughts, fears, and desires.

Dream work requires patience and practice. The more attention and value you give to your dreams, the more accessible and insightful they will become. It's also a deeply personal journey; what works for one person may not work for another. Experiment with different techniques and find what best suits your path to psychic development.

Dream work is a significant step in the psychic voyage, offering profound insights and opportunities for growth. By understanding and interpreting your dreams, engaging in lucid dreaming, and applying the messages and lessons from your dreams, you can enhance your psychic abilities and deepen your connection to the unseen realm.

PSYCHIC ETHICS AND RESPONSIBILITY

ETHICAL CONSIDERATIONS

In the realm of psychic development and practice, ethics stand as a cornerstone ensuring the integrity, respect, and trust between psychics and those they guide. Let's explore the core ethical considerations that psychic practitioners must navigate to maintain the sanctity of their work.

Ethical Responsibilities and Core Principles

The ethical framework for psychics revolves around key principles that ensure the welfare of clients while upholding the credibility of psychic practices:

- **Confidentiality and Privacy**: Psychics are entrusted with sensitive information, making it paramount to protect client confidentiality and privacy at all times. This trust forms the basis of a secure and respectful relationship between the psychic and the client.

- **Informed Consent**: Prior to any session, psychics should clearly explain the process, purpose, and potential outcomes, ensuring clients have a thorough understanding and agreement before proceeding.

- **Honesty and Integrity**: Providing readings with honesty, refraining from making unfounded promises, and acknowledging the limitations of psychic abilities are essential to maintaining integrity within the practice.

- **Avoiding Exploitation**: Psychics must avoid exploiting clients' vulnerabilities for financial, emotional, or any other gain. Upholding professionalism and objectivity prevents the misuse of the psychic-client relationship.

- **Professional Boundaries**: Establishing clear boundaries ensures the psychic-client interaction remains professional, preventing personal biases or relationships from influencing the guidance provided.

Ethical Concerns and Challenges

The psychic practice also faces ethical concerns that require vigilance and commitment to ethical conduct to address effectively:

- **Fraudulent Practices**: The psychic community is challenged by individuals who engage in deceitful practices. It's the responsibility of ethical psychics to help educate the public on identifying genuine psychic guidance.

- **Manipulation and Control**: Ethical psychics must

navigate the fine line between offering guidance and influencing clients' decisions, ensuring respect for clients' autonomy and free will.

- **Psychic Dependency**: Encouraging clients to make independent decisions and not overly rely on psychic readings for life choices is crucial to prevent dependency.

- **Financial Exploitation**: Transparent pricing and avoiding undue pressure on clients for additional services help in preventing financial exploitation.

- **Psychological Harm**: Considering the potential emotional impact of readings, psychics should approach sensitive topics with care and offer resources for further support if needed.

Vetting Process of Psychics

The credibility and skills of psychics are crucial, necessitating a thorough vetting process. This process assesses a psychic's background, abilities, and adherence to ethical standards. Rigorous vetting safeguards clients from fraudulent or unqualified practitioners and upholds the integrity of psychic services.

Avoiding Dependency and Promoting Skepticism

Ethical psychics discourage dependency, advising clients to view psychic insights as one of many tools for personal decision-making. Encouraging skepticism and critical thinking, they remind clients and themselves that psychic readings offer perspectives, not absolute answers.

Health and Legal Boundaries

Psychics must recognize the limits of their practice, refraining from offering medical, legal, or financial advice. Acknowledging the boundaries of psychic abilities ensures respect for professional fields and protects clients from potentially harmful misinformation.

Cultural Sensitivity and Personal Growth

An ethical psychic practice involves respecting cultural diversity and avoiding stereotypes. Psychics should focus on facilitating personal growth and self-awareness, empowering clients through their readings.

Ensuring Ethical Practice

To uphold ethical standards, psychics are encouraged to engage in continuous education, self-reflection, and professional development. Adherence to codes of ethics provided by reputable psychic organizations, participation in training programs, and peer discussions are instrumental in fostering ethical conduct. Regular self-reflection and supervision can also support psychics in navigating ethical dilemmas and maintaining their commitment to ethical practice.

By adhering to these ethical guidelines and responsibilities, psychics can provide their services in a manner that respects the client's well-being, autonomy, and the sacred trust inherent in the psychic-client relationship. This ethical approach not only enhances the integrity and credibility of psychic practices but also ensures that the psychic voyage remains a beneficial and empowering experience for all involved.

SETTING
BOUNDARIES

For individuals with heightened psychic sensitivity, navigating everyday life can present unique challenges and opportunities. Psychic sensitivity, or the ability to perceive and process a broader spectrum of sensory input, can lead to profound insights and connections but also requires careful management to prevent overwhelm. Setting boundaries is a crucial skill in this process, allowing those with psychic abilities to protect their energy and maintain well-being.

Understanding Psychic Sensitivity

Psychic sensitivity manifests in various forms, including heightened intuition, empathic abilities, and clairvoyant experiences. This sensitivity can enrich life with deep emotional connections and spiritual insights but also expose individuals to intense and sometimes overwhelming experiences of others' emotions and energies.

Understanding the Need for Boundaries

Empaths, by nature, are emotional sponges, absorbing feelings from their environment. This heightened sensitivity, while a gift, necessitates the development of robust emotional boundaries to prevent compassion fatigue and emotional overload. Unlike the common misconception, setting boundaries does not equate to erecting emotional barriers.

Instead, it involves installing a selective filter to manage what emotional and energetic stimuli you allow into your space.

Physical Boundaries

Creating physical space that feels safe and nurturing is vital. This may involve spending time in nature, creating a personal sanctuary for retreat, or using protective crystals or amulets. Physical boundaries also include being mindful of one's presence in large groups or public spaces, where energies can be more chaotic.

Emotional and Energetic Boundaries

Learning to distinguish between one's own emotions and those picked up from others is a critical aspect of setting emotional and energetic boundaries. Techniques such as grounding, centering, and shielding can help manage emotional overflow and prevent taking on external energies.

Strategies for Setting Boundaries

1. **Tune into Your Feelings**: Begin by regularly checking in with yourself to understand your emotional state.

Recognizing your feelings helps in identifying when you're taking on too much from others.

2. **Define Your Emotional Limits**: Determine what you can emotionally handle and identify situations or individuals that drain you. Establishing clear limits is crucial for self-preservation.

3. **Express Your Needs Verbally**: Communication is key in boundary setting. Clearly articulate your needs and limits to others to avoid misunderstandings and ensure your boundaries are respected.

4. **Practice Assertiveness**: Learning to say "no" is vital. Assertiveness allows you to stand up for yourself without feeling guilty for prioritizing your well-being.

5. **Engage in Regular Self-care**: Incorporate self-

care practices into your routine to recharge and reinforce the boundaries you've set. This not only strengthens your resilience but also supports your psychic and emotional health.

Grounding Techniques

Grounding techniques reconnect an individual with the earth's stabilizing energy. Practices such as walking barefoot on the ground, meditation focused on rooting oneself to the earth, or visualizing energy flowing out of the body into the ground can help discharge excess energy.

Centering and Shielding

Centering involves aligning with one's core essence, creating a sense of inner stability. Shielding is the practice of visualizing a protective barrier around oneself, which can be imagined as a sphere of light or a cocoon enveloping the body, serving to filter out unwanted energies.

Social Boundaries

Setting social boundaries involves being selective about the company one keeps and the environments one chooses to engage with. It may mean declining invitations to events that feel energetically overwhelming or limiting time spent in energetically taxing situations.

Communication Boundaries

Communicating needs and limits to others is essential. This might involve explaining one's sensitivity to close friends and family, setting expectations about availability, and expressing when a situation becomes too taxing.

Digital and Media Boundaries

The digital world, with its constant flow of information and emotional content, can be particularly challenging. Setting boundaries around media consumption and screen time is crucial for managing psychic sensitivity.

Self-Care and Personal Development

Engaging in regular self-care practices supports well-being and strengthens the capacity to maintain boundaries. This includes activities that nourish the body, mind, and spirit, such as yoga, meditation, creative pursuits, and spending time in nature.

When Boundaries Are Challenged

Not everyone will respect your boundaries, which can be a valuable indicator of the health of your relationships. Those who value and respect your needs will adhere to your boundaries, while others may resist or challenge them. Persisting in setting and enforcing your boundaries, even in the face of resistance, is essential for your well-being and the authenticity of your relationships.

Seeking Support

Building a support network of understanding individuals who respect one's boundaries and sensitivity is invaluable. This might include friends, family, or a community of like-minded individuals who share similar experiences.

Setting boundaries is an ongoing process that requires self-awareness, communication, and assertiveness. For empaths and individuals with heightened psychic sensitivity, boundaries are not a luxury but a necessity. By managing what you energetically and emotionally engage with, you can protect your well-being, deepen your connections, and navigate the world without becoming overwhelmed. As you practice boundary setting, remember that it is a form of self-love and respect, enabling you to use your psychic abilities in a balanced and healthy way.

THE RESPONSIBILITY OF INSIGHT - HANDLING PSYCHIC INFORMATION RESPONSIBLY

Handling sensitive or distressing information responsibly is a critical aspect of psychic practice, emphasizing the importance of ethical considerations, emotional preparedness, and maintaining confidentiality. Psychics find themselves in unique positions, holding delicate information about their clients' lives. Let's explore the multifaceted approach psychics employ to navigate these challenges, ensuring a supportive and respectful environment during readings.

Encouraging Self-Empowerment

The primary goal of a psychic reading should be to empower the client, enabling them to tap into their own inner wisdom and intuition. This involves shifting the focus from dependency on the psychic's insights to fostering the client's self-discovery and autonomy. Techniques such as reflective journaling and creative visualization can be introduced post-reading, allowing clients to explore and integrate insights on their own terms. This approach not only respects the client's autonomy but also supports their journey towards self-empowerment and personal growth.

Emotional Preparedness and Supportive Environment

Psychics must be emotionally prepared to handle sensitive information, acknowledging that clients may share deep emotions, traumatic experiences, or painful memories. Creating a safe and supportive environment is crucial, requiring psychics to build rapport, actively listen, and validate clients' emotions, fostering a space where clients feel comfortable and respected.

Empathy, Compassion, and Communication

Utilizing empathy and compassion allows psychics to connect with clients on a profound level, providing support that is genuinely empathetic and tailored to individual needs. Understanding clients' emotional states before delving into sensitive topics is key, as is providing emotional validation. Techniques for delivering sensitive information include using gentle language, metaphors, and analogies to convey messages without causing distress, and employing active listening skills to ensure clients feel heard and understood.

Integrating Intuition and Sensitivity

Psychics rely on intuition and sensitivity to navigate the energetic and emotional aspects of clients' situations, providing insights that align with clients' needs while remaining sensitive to their emotional state. Establishing boundaries and practicing emotional self-care are vital for psychics to maintain their well-being and provide effective support without becoming overwhelmed.

Consent and Boundaries

Consent is paramount in psychic readings. It ensures that clients are aware of and agree to the reading's scope, respecting their right to privacy and autonomy. Ethical psychics make it a point to obtain explicit consent before delving into sensitive topics, thereby protecting the client's privacy and ensuring that the reading does not cross personal boundaries. Additionally, setting clear boundaries regarding the topics covered, the duration of the session, and maintaining professional decorum helps safeguard both the psychic's and the client's well-being.

Ethical Considerations and Confidentiality

Ethics play a significant role in handling sensitive information. Psychics are responsible for maintaining client confidentiality, ensuring privacy, and building trust. By recognizing their personal limits and finding a balance between empathy and detachment, psychics can support their clients while preserving their own emotional health. Continuous professional development and support are encouraged to enhance psychics' ability to address sensitive topics effectively.

Establishing Client-Psychic Rapport

Creating a strong rapport between the psychic and the client is foundational to a fruitful reading. This rapport is built on active listening, open and honest communication, and a clear understanding of the client's needs and boundaries. By explaining the reading process and the meanings of the cards in a way that resonates personally with the client, psychics can facilitate a more engaging and insightful experience. Such a relationship fosters an atmosphere of trust and safety, enabling deeper exploration and more meaningful insights.

Navigating Emotional Reactions

Psychics may encounter emotional reactions from clients, such as tears or breakdowns, during readings. Providing a comforting presence, offering tissues, and guiding clients towards self-care practices can aid in emotional healing. By assisting clients in understanding and processing their emotions, psychics facilitate healthy emotional release.

Continuous Learning and Professionalism

An ethical psychic is committed to continuous learning and professional development. This includes staying abreast of best practices, deepening their understanding of psychic work, and refining their skills in interpretation and client communication. Professional boundaries are essential; they prevent misuse of the reader-client relationship and ensure that the focus remains on the client's well-being.

Handling sensitive or distressing information in psychic

readings requires a comprehensive approach that includes emotional preparedness, empathy, ethical considerations, and maintaining confidentiality. By adhering to these ethical principles, psychics and tarot readers can ensure that their practices serve as a positive and empowering tool in their clients' lives. Ethical conduct not only enhances the credibility and integrity of psychic readings but also fosters a trusting and respectful relationship between psychics and their clients, ultimately contributing to the clients' personal growth and self-understanding.

OVERCOMING
CHALLENGES

DEALING WITH PSYCHIC BLOCKS

Psychic blocks are barriers within the mind that hinder the flow of psychic information and intuitive insights. These blocks can stem from various sources, including emotional trauma, fear, skepticism, and physical or mental exhaustion. Identifying and overcoming these obstacles is crucial for psychic development.

Understanding Psychic Blocks

Psychic blocks manifest as a feeling of being disconnected from one's intuitive senses. Common symptoms include a sudden lack of clarity, difficulty in accessing psychic abilities that were previously available, or an overwhelming sense of doubt or fear when attempting to tap into one's psychic potential. These blocks can be temporary, fluctuating with one's emotional and physical state, or more persistent, requiring deliberate effort to overcome.

Common Causes of Psychic Blocks

- **Emotional Trauma**: Past emotional traumas can create barriers to psychic abilities, as the subconscious mind may seek to protect the individual from reliving painful experiences.

- **Fear**: Fear of the unknown, fear of being wrong, or fear of judgment from others can severely limit psychic development.

- **Skepticism**: While healthy skepticism can be beneficial, an overly skeptical mindset can block psychic intuition by fostering doubt and disbelief.

- **Physical and Mental Exhaustion**: A tired mind and body cannot effectively channel psychic energies. Rest and self-care are essential for maintaining psychic sensitivity.

Strategies for Overcoming Psychic Blocks

- **Meditation and Mindfulness**: Regular meditation can help quiet the mind, reduce fear and skepticism, and promote a state of openness and receptivity to psychic information.

- **Healing Emotional Traumas**: Seeking therapeutic support to heal emotional wounds can remove significant barriers to psychic development.

- **Building Confidence**: Engaging in practices that build psychic skills in a supportive environment can gradually overcome fears and bolster confidence in one's abilities.

- **Energy Work**: Techniques such as Reiki, yoga, or tai chi can help clear energy blockages and enhance psychic flow.

- **Journaling**: Keeping a journal of psychic experiences, even unsuccessful attempts, can provide insights into patterns of blocks and progress made over time.

- **Nature Connection**: Spending time in nature can recharge psychic energy and provide a grounding effect, facilitating a clearer psychic connection.

Recognizing Progress

Overcoming psychic blocks is a process that requires patience and self-compassion. Progress may not always be linear, and setbacks are a natural part of growth. Celebrating small victories and maintaining a positive, open mindset can encourage continued development and eventual mastery over these blocks.

Psychic blocks, while challenging, are not insurmountable. They serve as an opportunity for introspection and growth, pushing individuals to confront and heal underlying issues. By addressing these blocks, psychics can unlock deeper levels of intuition, clarity, and connection to the unseen realm, enhancing their psychic journey.

COPING WITH PSYCHIC SENSITIVITY

Psychic sensitivity, or heightened awareness to psychic stimuli, can be both a gift and a challenge. For those developing their psychic abilities, managing this sensitivity is crucial to avoid feeling overwhelmed by the energies and emotions of others and their environment.

Recognizing Psychic Sensitivity

Psychic sensitivity manifests in various ways, such as feeling suddenly drained in crowded places, experiencing strong intuitive hunches, or having vivid dreams that offer insights into real-life situations. Sensitives might also find themselves affected by the moods and emotions of others, picking up on subtleties that others miss.

Grounding Techniques

Grounding is essential for psychics to release excess energy and maintain a balanced state. Techniques include:

- Walking barefoot on the earth to connect with its stabilizing energy.
- Visualization practices, imagining roots growing from one's feet into the ground.
- Engaging in mindfulness or meditation to center oneself.

Shielding Practices

Shielding involves creating a psychic barrier to protect oneself from unwanted energies. This can be visualized as a bubble or shield of light encasing the body, specifically intended to block out negative or overwhelming energies while allowing positive energies to enter.

Energy Cleansing

Regular energy cleansing helps remove accumulated negative energy and maintain psychic hygiene. This can be done through:

- Smudging with sage or palo santo.

- Taking salt baths to purify the aura.

- Using crystals like black tourmaline or selenite to absorb and neutralize negative energies.

Emotional Regulation

Managing emotions is vital for psychics, as their sensitivity can lead to emotional overload. Techniques for emotional regulation include:

- Identifying and expressing emotions in a healthy way, such as through journaling or art.

- Practicing self-compassion and understanding that it's okay to feel deeply.

- Seeking support from like-minded individuals or a

mentor experienced in psychic development.

Setting Boundaries

Psychic sensitives must learn to set boundaries to protect their energy. This means learning to say no to situations or individuals that drain their energy and being mindful of their limits in giving and receiving psychic information.

Nurturing Physical Health

A healthy body supports a healthy psychic mind. Adequate sleep, a nutritious diet, regular exercise, and hydration are all important. These physical practices support psychic resilience and prevent burnout.

Developing a Support Network

Connecting with others who understand psychic sensitivity can provide valuable support, advice, and understanding. Whether through online communities or local groups, finding a network of like-minded individuals can be incredibly affirming.

Recognizing the Gift

While challenging, psychic sensitivity is a profound gift that allows for deep connections with others, the environment, and the unseen world. Embracing this gift involves accepting and valuing the sensitivity as a key part of one's psychic journey, using it to foster empathy, intuition, and a deeper understanding of the world.

Continuous Learning

Engaging in continuous learning about psychic development and sensitivity management can provide new strategies for coping and thriving. Reading, workshops, and courses can all contribute to a deeper understanding and mastery of one's psychic abilities.

Coping with psychic sensitivity is a dynamic and ongoing process that involves a combination of grounding, shielding, emotional regulation, and community support. By implementing these strategies, individuals can manage their sensitivity effectively, turning what may seem like a vulnerability into a powerful tool for psychic development and a deeper connection with the world.

WHEN PSYCHIC DEVELOPMENT FEELS OVERWHELMING: FINDING BALANCE AND SUPPORT

In the pursuit of psychic development, individuals may encounter moments of overwhelm due to the intensified sensitivity to energies, heightened emotions, and the influx of psychic information. Here are presented practical strategies to navigate these overwhelming feelings, ensuring a balanced approach to psychic growth and well-being.

Managing Psychic Sensitivity

For those experiencing an amplified spectrum of reality, grounding and centering exercises are invaluable tools. Grounding connects one with the Earth's energy, fostering stability, while centering aligns one's energy, promoting internal balance. Together, these practices aid in managing psychic abilities in a controlled manner. The chakra system, acting as filters for psychic and physical realms, requires balance for effective energy flow. Traumatic experiences can disrupt this balance, leading to both physical and emotional issues alongside heightened psychic sensitivity. Addressing these traumas through therapy, energy healing, and somatic practices is crucial for restoring balance.

Recognizing Psychic Overwhelm

Psychic overwhelm manifests through several signs, including heightened sensitivity, emotional overload, depleted energy levels, difficulty concentrating, physical symptoms like headaches and digestive issues, and feelings of disconnection. Identifying these signs early can help individuals take necessary steps to mitigate overwhelm and restore equilibrium.

Practical Tips for Nervous System Overwhelm

Engaging in physical activities such as yoga or tai chi can alleviate tension and promote energetic flow. Taking time for decompression, through meditation or nature walks, allows the nervous system to process and rebalance. Progressive relaxation techniques, focusing on tensing and releasing muscle groups, offer immediate relief from physical manifestations of stress. Additionally, seeking guidance from a spiritual teacher or mentor can provide personalized support and tools to navigate psychic development more effectively.

General Strategies to Calm Down When Overwhelmed

Deep breathing exercises can counteract rapid, shallow breathing associated with stress, fostering a sense of calm. Practicing mindfulness, by being present and observing thoughts without judgment, helps in regaining focus and tranquility. Taking short breaks from stressors, engaging in physical exercise, and connecting with supportive individuals can also significantly reduce feelings of overwhelm. Organizing tasks and prioritizing self-care are essential steps in managing and reducing overwhelming sensations.

By integrating these strategies into daily routines, individuals can better navigate the challenges associated with psychic development, ensuring a journey that is not only enriching but also balanced and sustainable.

INTEGRATING PSYCHIC ABILITIES INTO DAILY LIFE

LIVING WITH PSYCHIC ABILITIES: INCORPORATING PSYCHIC INSIGHTS INTO DAILY ROUTINES

Incorporating psychic insights into daily routines involves integrating your heightened awareness and intuitive skills into every aspect of your life, from personal decision-making to interactions with others, enhancing the quality of your daily experience.

Mindful Morning Practices

Begin each day with a mindful practice to set the tone for heightened psychic awareness. Engage in meditation, journaling, or a brief tarot or oracle card reading. These practices help in grounding your energy and tuning into your intuitive senses, providing guidance for the day ahead.

Intuitive Decision-Making

Apply your psychic abilities to make decisions, big and small. Before making choices, take a moment to quiet your mind and listen to your intuition. This can be as simple as selecting what to wear based on your energy reading for the day or as significant as making career decisions guided by your inner voice.

Psychic Protection Rituals

As you step out into the world, employ psychic protection rituals to shield your energy. Visualization techniques, such as imagining a protective bubble or cloak of light around you, can safeguard your psychic sensitivity from overwhelming external energies.

Enhanced Communication

Use your psychic abilities to enhance communication in your personal and professional relationships. Pay attention to non-verbal cues and the energy you perceive from others. This can lead to deeper understanding and more meaningful connections.

Mindful Eating and Health

Incorporate psychic insights into your health and wellness routine by intuitively selecting foods and activities that resonate with your body's needs. Listen to your body's psychic cues about what nourishes and depletes you, adjusting your diet and exercise accordingly.

Energy Checks Throughout the Day

Regularly check in with your energy levels and the state of your aura or chakras. This can be done through brief meditative pauses to realign and cleanse your energy, ensuring you remain balanced and centered.

Integrating Nature and Environment

Connect with nature to enhance your psychic abilities. Spend time outdoors to ground yourself and clear your energy. The natural world provides a powerful backdrop for psychic development and can offer profound insights and rejuvenation.

Evening Reflection and Gratitude

End your day with a reflective practice, reviewing the insights and guidance received through your psychic abilities. Acknowledge the ways in which your psychic insights have enriched your day, fostering a sense of gratitude and openness to the continued guidance of your intuition.

Dream Work

As you prepare for sleep, set the intention to receive psychic insights through your dreams. Keep a dream journal beside your bed to record any significant dreams upon waking, as these can offer valuable messages and guidance from your subconscious and the spiritual realm.

Continuous Learning and Adaptation

Embrace the journey of living with psychic abilities as an ongoing learning process. Be open to adapting your daily routines as your psychic skills evolve, incorporating new practices and discarding those that no longer serve your growth.

Living with psychic abilities is a dynamic and enriching experience, deeply woven into the fabric of your daily life. By mindfully integrating your psychic insights into your routines, you create a life that is not only guided by deep inner wisdom but also aligned with your highest potential.

PSYCHIC ABILITIES IN RELATIONSHIPS: NAVIGATING INTERPERSONAL DYNAMICS

Psychic abilities significantly influence relationships and interpersonal dynamics by deepening connections, enhancing empathy, and facilitating a deeper understanding of others. These abilities, or psychic senses, include clairvoyance, clairsentience, clairaudience, and claircognizance, among others. Initially, everyone is born with these psychic senses, but they often become dormant over time. By reactivating and developing these senses through practices such as meditation, journaling, and spending time in nature, individuals can regain their innate psychic capabilities.

In the context of relationships, psychic abilities allow individuals to sense beyond the surface level of interactions, picking up on non-verbal cues, emotional energies, and even unspoken thoughts of others. This can lead to a more empathetic and understanding approach to communication and conflict resolution. Psychic insights can also preemptively identify potential issues or misunderstandings before they escalate, fostering a harmonious environment.

Moreover, psychic development encourages individuals to connect with their intuition, guiding them in making decisions that are not only beneficial for themselves but also supportive of their relationships. By tapping into one's psychic senses, it becomes possible to navigate interpersonal dynamics with a heightened sense of awareness and sensitivity to the energies around them.

Furthermore, psychic abilities can play a crucial role in spiritual growth within relationships. By exploring psychic development together, partners can embark on a shared journey of spiritual exploration, deepening their bond and mutual understanding. This shared path can lead to a more profound, soulful connection, transcending the mundane aspects of the relationship and exploring the depths of spiritual and emotional intimacy.

In essence, integrating psychic abilities into relationships transforms the way individuals relate to one another. It shifts the focus from ego-driven interactions to a more heart-centered, intuitive communication. By harnessing psychic senses, individuals can create relationships that are not only emotionally fulfilling but also spiritually enriching, offering a deeper sense of connection and understanding.

PSYCHIC DEVELOPMENT AND CAREER: UTILIZING PSYCHIC SKILLS IN PROFESSIONAL LIFE

In the modern professional landscape, the integration of psychic abilities into career development and business strategies has gained significant traction. Recognized not only for personal growth, psychic skills are increasingly utilized in various professional fields, offering unique insights and competitive advantages. Let's delve into how psychic abilities can be harnessed to enhance career prospects, improve business operations, and make impactful decisions in the corporate world.

Psychic Abilities in the Workplace

Psychic skills, such as intuition, clairvoyance, and energy reading, can play a pivotal role in the workplace. These abilities enable professionals to sense undercurrents in business environments, predict market trends, and understand non-verbal communication among colleagues and clients. Psychic abilities can also aid in conflict resolution, by sensing the emotions and intentions of all parties involved, leading to more empathetic and effective solutions.

Career Paths for Psychic Abilities

There are numerous career paths where psychic abilities can be directly applied or serve as a complementary skill set. Some of these include:

- **Business Consultants and Coaches**: Leveraging psychic insights to guide strategic planning, leadership development, and organizational change.

- **Creative Industries**: Utilizing intuition to enhance artistic expression, design, and innovation.

- **Health and Wellness**: Applying energy healing techniques and intuitive counseling to promote physical and emotional well-being.

- **Law Enforcement**: Assisting in solving crimes through psychic detective work, though controversial and subject to debate regarding its efficacy.

- **Marketing and Branding**: Employing psychic skills to understand consumer behavior and predict future trends.

Developing Psychic Skills for Professional Success

Enhancing psychic abilities can lead to significant professional development and success. Meditation, mindfulness, and engaging with nature are foundational practices that foster psychic growth. Additionally, training programs and workshops focused on psychic development can provide structured pathways for honing these skills.

Psychic Skills in Decision Making

Integrating psychic abilities into decision-making processes allows for a more holistic approach to navigating career challenges and opportunities. Trusting one's intuition can lead to innovative solutions and strategic foresight, often resulting in better outcomes than relying on data and conventional wisdom alone.

Ethical Considerations

When applying psychic abilities in professional settings, ethical considerations are paramount. Respecting privacy, maintaining integrity, and ensuring that psychic insights are used responsibly and for the greater good are essential principles to uphold.

Psychic development offers profound opportunities for career advancement and professional enrichment. By understanding and integrating psychic skills into their work, individuals can access deeper insights, foster more meaningful connections, and achieve greater success in their professional lives.

COMMUNITY AND SHARED EXPERIENCES

FINDING YOUR PSYCHIC COMMUNITY: CONNECTING WITH LIKE-MINDED INDIVIDUALS

Finding a psychic community that resonates with you can be a transformative experience, offering support, understanding, and opportunities to grow in your psychic development journey. A psychic community consists of individuals who share an interest in exploring and developing their psychic abilities, providing a space for learning, exchange, and validation of psychic experiences.

Seeking Psychic Communities

The first step in finding your psychic community is to identify what you're looking for. Are you interested in a specific aspect of psychic development, such as mediumship, energy healing, or tarot reading? Knowing your interests will help you narrow down the search.

Local Workshops and Events

Attending local workshops, classes, and events is a great way to meet others interested in psychic development. These gatherings provide a physical space to connect, share experiences, and learn from one another. Check community bulletin boards, spiritual shops, and online event platforms for listings.

Online Forums and Social Media

The digital age has made it easier to find communities that share your interests. Online forums, social media groups, and psychic development websites offer platforms to ask questions, share experiences, and connect with others from around the world. Platforms like Reddit, Facebook, and specialized psychic development sites are good places to start.

Psychic Fairs and Conventions

Psychic fairs and conventions bring together practitioners, learners, and enthusiasts of psychic arts. These events are excellent opportunities to explore various aspects of psychic development, discover new tools and resources, and connect with a broader community.

Spiritual Centers and Metaphysical Shops

Many spiritual centers and metaphysical shops host regular meetings, circles, or groups focused on psychic development and spiritual growth. These spaces often provide a welcoming environment for those looking to deepen their psychic abilities and connect with like-minded individuals.

Creating Your Community

If you're unable to find a community that fits your needs, consider starting your own. Hosting meet-ups, study groups, or online forums can attract others with similar interests. This initiative not only helps you find your community but also positions you as an active participant in your psychic development journey.

Benefits of Joining a Psychic Community

Joining a psychic community offers numerous benefits, including:

- **Support and Understanding**: Being part of a community provides emotional support and understanding from individuals who share similar experiences and challenges.

- **Knowledge and Learning**: Communities offer a wealth of knowledge and opportunities for learning through workshops, discussions, and shared experiences.

- **Validation and Confidence**: Sharing your experiences with others who understand and believe in psychic phenomena can validate your experiences and boost your confidence in your abilities.

- **Networking and Opportunities**: Being part of a psychic community opens up opportunities for collaboration, mentorship, and professional development within the field of psychic and spiritual work.

Maintaining Ethical Standards

It's important to approach psychic communities with discernment and maintain ethical standards. Respect for privacy, consent in psychic readings, and an open-minded but critical approach to psychic phenomena are essential.

Finding your psychic community can significantly enhance your journey in psychic development. Whether through local events, online platforms, or creating your own group, connecting with like-minded individuals offers a sense of belonging, opportunities for growth, and a deeper exploration of the unseen realm.

SHARING AND VALIDATING EXPERIENCES

In the journey of psychic development, sharing and validating experiences with others is not just beneficial—it's essential. Let's delve into the profound impact that sharing personal psychic experiences can have on individuals and communities alike.

The Power of Sharing

Sharing psychic experiences with others serves multiple purposes. It provides a platform for validation, reduces feelings of isolation, and fosters a sense of belonging. When individuals open up about their psychic journeys, they often find that others have had similar experiences. This shared understanding can be incredibly affirming, offering reassurance that one's experiences are not merely figments of imagination but part of a broader, shared reality.

Validation Through Community

Engaging with a community or mentor experienced in psychic development can be transformative. It offers not only guidance but also reassurance and validation. Being part of a community allows for the exchange of experiences, learning from others, and growing in a supportive environment. Such interactions help in overcoming common obstacles like skepticism and overwhelm, by balancing openness with groundedness and providing coping strategies through grounding techniques and shared experiences.

The Role of Personal Experiences

Personal stories of psychic development, such as early signs of psychic abilities in childhood, interactions with spirits, and profound moments of astral projection, illustrate the diversity and depth of psychic experiences. These narratives underscore the importance of sharing, as they can enlighten, inspire, and validate others on their psychic journeys. For instance, childhood experiences of psychic phenomena, such as seeing spirits or experiencing past life memories, highlight  the natural psychic abilities that many possess from a young age. Sharing these stories helps demystify psychic experiences and encourages others to explore their own abilities without fear or skepticism.

Enhancing Relationships

On a more intimate level, shared psychic experiences can significantly deepen personal relationships. When individuals share these moments with loved ones, they create unique bonds and a shared history that enriches their relationship. Such experiences offer a mutual understanding and trust, building a stronger, more connected relationship. Whether it's navigating psychic development together or supporting each other's psychic journey, these shared moments become integral to the relationship's fabric, enhancing understanding, trust, and emotional intimacy.

Sharing and validating psychic experiences is crucial for personal growth and community building within the psychic development journey. It encourages a deeper understanding of oneself and others, fosters connections, and helps in navigating the complexities of psychic abilities. By embracing shared experiences, individuals can find strength in community, deepen relationships, and progress confidently on their psychic voyage.

LEARNING FROM OTHERS

The path to psychic development is enriched through the wisdom and experiences of those who have traversed it before us. Learning from experienced psychics and mediums offers invaluable insights and lessons that can accelerate personal growth, enhance psychic abilities, and deepen spiritual connections. Let's explore the multifaceted journey of learning from others, highlighting the benefits of mentorship, the importance of community, and the transformative impact of shared wisdom on psychic development.

Mentorship from experienced psychics and mediums is a cornerstone of psychic development. These mentors provide tailored guidance, support, and feedback that is crucial for navigating the complexities of psychic abilities. They offer practical techniques for cultivating psychic skills such as clairvoyance, clairaudience, and clairsentience, and share strategies for overcoming common challenges. Through mentorship, individuals gain access to a wealth of knowledge and experience that can significantly shorten the learning curve and foster a deeper understanding of the psychic realm.

Community plays a vital role in psychic development. Joining psychic development groups, participating in workshops, and engaging in online forums creates opportunities for learning from a diverse group of practitioners. These communities offer a supportive environment where individuals can share their experiences, exchange tips, and validate their psychic

experiences. The collective wisdom of a community provides a broad spectrum of perspectives and practices, enriching the individual's journey and promoting a sense of belonging.

Learning from the experiences of others also involves understanding the ethical considerations and responsibilities that come with psychic abilities. Experienced psychics and mediums often share their insights on navigating the ethical dilemmas that can arise, emphasizing the importance of integrity, respect, and compassion in psychic practices. These lessons help individuals develop a strong ethical foundation, ensuring that their psychic abilities are used in a manner that is beneficial to themselves and others.

The journey of psychic development is also about continuous learning and growth. Engaging with the experiences of others opens the door to new techniques, practices, and areas of psychic exploration. It encourages an open-minded approach to psychic development, where individuals are always ready to expand their knowledge and refine their skills. This openness to learning from others fosters a dynamic and evolving psychic practice that remains responsive to the individual's growth and the changing landscape of psychic exploration.

Learning from experienced psychics and mediums enriches the psychic development journey in profound ways. It offers a blend of personalized guidance, community support, ethical grounding, and continuous learning that together create a powerful framework for unlocking psychic potential. By embracing the wisdom of those who have walked the path before, individuals can navigate the psychic voyage with greater confidence, clarity, and connection to the unseen realm.

CONTINUING THE
PSYCHIC JOURNEY

LIFELONG LEARNING

Lifelong learning in the context of psychic development is an essential journey that extends beyond the acquisition of initial skills and insights. It encompasses continuous exploration, growth, and adaptation, ensuring psychics not only maintain their abilities but also expand them in response to evolving spiritual landscapes. Let's explore the facets of lifelong learning, emphasizing its importance for psychics at all stages of their journey.

One of the core aspects of lifelong learning is the pursuit of knowledge. This includes staying informed about advancements in psychic practices, understanding new theories in the metaphysical realm, and exploring related disciplines such as psychology, philosophy, and quantum physics. Such knowledge enriches a psychic's understanding of their abilities and the world they navigate, offering deeper insights into their experiences and those of the people they help.

Another crucial element is skill enhancement. Lifelong learning involves regular practice and refinement of psychic abilities. Techniques such as meditation, energy work, and divination are not static; they evolve as the practitioner grows. Engaging in ongoing training, whether through workshops, courses, or self-study, helps in honing these skills. It also opens the door to discovering new psychic talents and improving the effectiveness of existing ones.

Adaptability and openness to change are vital for psychic development. The psychic realm is dynamic, with new methodologies and practices emerging over time. Lifelong learners are open to integrating these changes into their practice, allowing them to stay relevant and effective. This adaptability also prepares psychics to navigate their own spiritual transformations and the shifts in energy they perceive in the world around them.

Personal growth is an integral part of lifelong learning. Psychic abilities are deeply connected to the practitioner's inner world. Therefore, personal development—such as cultivating self-awareness, managing ego, and dealing with personal issues—directly impacts psychic proficiency. Lifelong learning in this area involves continuous self-reflection, emotional intelligence, and spiritual growth.

Community engagement also plays a significant role. Learning from and with others—whether through psychic development groups, mentorships, or collaborative projects—

provides valuable perspectives and insights. It fosters a sense of belonging and contributes to the collective knowledge of the psychic community. Sharing experiences and wisdom with others not only aids in the individual's growth but also uplifts the entire psychic field.

Lastly, the ethical dimension of psychic work necessitates ongoing attention. Lifelong learning includes understanding and applying ethical standards in all psychic practices. This involves consent, confidentiality, and the responsible use of psychic insights. As society's views on ethics evolve, so too must the psychic's approach to these issues.

Lifelong learning in psychic development is a multidimensional journey that enriches the practitioner's abilities, enhances their service to others, and deepens their understanding of the universe. It is an endless voyage of discovery that promises growth, transformation, and an ever-expanding connection to the unseen realm.

EXPANDING HORIZONS

In the realm of psychic development, expanding horizons refers to the continuous exploration of new areas and dimensions within the psychic and spiritual landscapes. This journey involves venturing beyond traditional practices and embracing innovative methods, thereby enriching one's psychic abilities and deepening spiritual understanding. Let's explore various avenues through which psychics can broaden their horizons, including emerging psychic disciplines, interdisciplinary approaches, and the integration of technology in psychic practices.

Emerging Psychic Disciplines: The psychic domain is ever-evolving, with new disciplines emerging as understanding and experiences within the field expand. Practices such as energy matrix reading, quantum jumping, and digital mediumship are gaining traction. These disciplines offer fresh perspectives and techniques, providing psychics with new tools for exploration and insight. Engaging with these emerging areas not only enhances one's psychic repertoire but also contributes to the collective knowledge of psychic phenomena.

Interdisciplinary Approaches: Expanding horizons in psychic development also involves integrating knowledge and techniques from various disciplines. This includes drawing insights from quantum physics, psychology, neurology, and cultural studies to enrich psychic practices. For instance, understanding the quantum theory of entanglement can

deepen insights into psychic connections, while psychological theories on consciousness can offer new ways to understand psychic experiences. This interdisciplinary approach fosters a more holistic understanding of psychic phenomena and its interaction with the physical world.

Technological Integration: The advent of technology offers novel ways to explore and practice psychic abilities. Virtual reality, for example, can simulate environments for astral projection practice, while biofeedback devices can help individuals learn to control their psychic energy more effectively. Online platforms and apps are also being developed to facilitate psychic learning and practice, connecting psychics across the globe and enabling the exchange of ideas and experiences. Embracing technology can thus significantly broaden the scope and reach of psychic practices.

Environmental and Cosmic Connections: Expanding horizons also involves exploring the psychic connections with the environment and the cosmos. This includes eco-psychic practices that deepen one's connection to the Earth and its energies, as well as cosmic psychism that explores the influence of celestial bodies and cosmic events on psychic abilities. These connections highlight the interdependence of all existence and the vastness of the psychic realm, inviting psychics to explore beyond the confines of the individual and the immediate.

Ethical and Philosophical Considerations: As psychics venture into new areas, ethical and philosophical considerations become increasingly important. This involves reflecting on the implications of psychic practices, the responsible use of psychic abilities, and the philosophical questions that arise from psychic experiences. Engaging with these considerations ensures that psychic practices remain grounded in integrity and contribute positively to individual and collective well-being.

Expanding horizons in psychic development is a dynamic and ongoing process. It invites psychics to remain curious, open-minded, and committed to growth. By exploring new disciplines, integrating interdisciplinary approaches, embracing technology, and connecting with the environment and cosmos, psychics can enrich their practice and contribute to the evolution of psychic understanding.

THE FUTURE
OF PSYCHIC
EXPLORATION

The future of psychic exploration is poised at the crossroads of tradition and innovation, marked by an expanding landscape that integrates emerging technologies, evolving societal attitudes, and a deeper scientific inquiry into the metaphysical realm. Let's delve into the anticipated trends and potential advancements that may shape the trajectory of psychic development and spiritual exploration in the years to come.

Technological Integration and Virtual Realities: The integration of virtual and augmented reality in psychic practices is a significant trend on the horizon. These technologies could transform traditional psychic services, enabling immersive experiences where clients and psychics interact within virtual spaces. This could deepen the intimacy and effectiveness of readings, extending the boundaries of psychic exploration to new, uncharted territories.

Growth of the Psychic Industry: The psychic industry is experiencing a resurgence, with a projected increase in market size driven by rising interest and disposable income. The industry's diversification into various sub-sectors, including astrology, aura reading, and mediumship, indicates a broadening of services that cater to a growing clientele seeking spiritual guidance. This growth is complemented by an increasing move towards online platforms, making psychic services more accessible to a global audience.

Emerging Psychic Disciplines: New areas of psychic practice are emerging, blending traditional psychic skills with contemporary insights from quantum physics and neuroscience. Innovations such as neurofeedback, audiovisual entrainment, and pulsed electromagnetic field therapy are being explored for their potential to enhance psychic abilities. These techniques aim to amplify psychic talents while fostering empathy, creativity, and mental clarity.

Cultural and Demographic Shifts: The demographic profile of those interested in psychic services is evolving, with younger generations showing increased openness to psychic and spiritual experiences. This shift is likely to influence the types of services offered and the modalities through which they are accessed, with a greater emphasis on digital and mobile platforms.

Scientific Inquiry and Psychic Phenomena: The relationship between psychic phenomena and scientific inquiry continues to evolve, with ongoing research into the quantum realm offering potential explanations for psychic insights. Parapsychology and studies into consciousness are gradually gaining mainstream recognition, suggesting a future where psychic phenomena may be more deeply understood through the lens of science.

Ethical and Philosophical Considerations: As the psychic field expands, ethical and philosophical considerations become increasingly important. The future of psychic exploration will likely involve a greater emphasis on ethical practices, transparency, and the responsible use of psychic abilities. This includes addressing concerns about exploitation and ensuring that psychic practices contribute positively to individual and societal well-being.

The future of psychic exploration is marked by a dynamic interplay between tradition and innovation, with technological advancements, scientific exploration, and changing societal attitudes shaping the path forward. As we venture into this future, the psychic journey promises to be one of continuous discovery, growth, and an ever-deepening understanding of the unseen realm.

THE END

Printed in Great Britain
by Amazon